My Buddy Butch

My Buddy Butch

Confessions of a New Dog Dad

Jeff Marginean

jemar entertainment, inc.

a jemar entertainment publication – softcover edition

www.jemarentertainment.com

MY BUDDY BUTCH is a trademark of JEMAR Entertainment, Inc.
MY BUDDY BUTCH™

My Buddy Butch – Confessions of a New Dog Dad. Copyright © 2008 by Jeffrey E. Marginean. All rights reserved. Printed in the United States of America. No part of this book may be used or reproduced in any manner whatsoever, either by copy or recording, without the expressed written consent of JEMAR Entertainment, Inc. and Jeff Marginean except in the case of brief quotations embodied in literary articles including reviews used in newsprint, magazine, and on-line.

JEMAR Entertainment publications may be purchased in quantity for educational, business, or sales incentive use. For information please write to: JEMAR Entertainment, Inc. Special Markets, P.O. Box 2946, North Canton, Ohio 44720-0946. Please see our Web site for email and phone contact inquiries.

Design by Jeff Marginean

Frisbee is a registered trademark of Wham-O, Inc.
Invisible Fence is a registered trademark of Invisible Fence, Inc.
Ford Ranger is a registered trademark of Ford Motor Company.
The Grammy Award® is a registered trademark of the National Academy for Recording Arts and Sciences.

ISBN-10: 0-9814621-0-3
ISBN-13: 978-0-9814621-0-3
Library of Congress Control Number: 2008920437

For Mom

Irene Marginean
(1925 – 2003)

CONTENTS

AUTHOR'S NOTE

This book is a work of nonfiction. It was written for the purpose of having a little fun, documenting an important part of my life, the beginning of Butch's new life, and hopefully transferring some of the knowledge that I have obtained while trying to do a good job of raising him. It contains opinions, reflections, and commentary on life, love, and learning to live with a new, hairy little addition to my world, from a single person's perspective. All of the people, places, and stories in this book are real although some of the names were changed. The situations, however unbelievable, did happen. I hope you have as much fun reading this as I had writing it!

PREFACE

I grew up in a relatively normal family, which consisted of Mom, Dad, and us four kids. I, being the youngest of the "brood," was constantly peppered with the obligatory, "You were spoiled!" from everyone while I was growing up. The closest to me in age was my sister Jeanne but there was still a substantial spread of eight years between us. Judy, Jim, Jeanne, and then me was, and still is, the order. And yes, OK, our names all start with J, how quaint. I've heard that a lot also over the years! Effectively, I was an only child, for a number of years, being the last one at home. With a large spread of years between us four, the others were out of the house and I was the last one left.

Dad was always interested in animals. He's always been interested in them and we used to watch animal shows together on TV every week. I can remember watching *Wild Kingdom* with Marlin Perkins and then Disney every Sunday night while growing up. I can also remember the stories about Mom sending Dad to the store to get a broom and Dad walking down the alley behind our house with a broom on one shoulder and a monkey on the other. He had purchased or borrowed the monkey to see what Mom's reaction would be. Well, as you can imagine, she took the broom from him and made him take the monkey back. I'm not sure if she just told him to take it back or actually chased him down the alley with the broom! Anyway, there were a myriad of stories that reflected Dad's love of animals. Knowing this, it was a natural course of events for my folks to eventually own a dog and they did, much to Mom's dismay. I think I inherited some of Dad's love of animals because, for as long as I have been on my own, I have entertained the thought of owning a dog. Having not had a dog since I was a kid, and being a single guy constantly on the run, I was a little leery about the logistics of taking care of a new dog or puppy and not being able to spend enough time with him or her. I had thought about it for many years and had gone through the bevy of easy-to-take-care-of pets; albeit the not-too-cuddly type.

I owned a parakeet that didn't do much but fly around and soil its food dish. I can't remember naming it although it's not likely it would have remembered its name anyway. I can't remember how long it lived but I did feel bad when it died. I buried it in the backyard and it was probably dug up and eaten by the first skunk or opossum that passed by. I also had a conure, which is like a small parrot. I named it Pepita, which was kind of stupid now that I think of it, even though it was from Central America or so I was told, but it was a female. Those babies aren't cheap. I probably had $1,700 wrapped up in a full-blown cage and setup. Being the tinkerer that I am, I had set up an elaborate playground for it with ladders, bells, mirrors, and the like, only to have it turned into sawdust. These birds' beaks are very strong and could probably crush or break your finger if it got hold of it. It could crack a small walnut with no problem at all. This made doing any kind of training precarious at best. I did manage to teach her how to give a kiss without having my eyes pecked out. It was amazing to watch and I did teach her some tricks but after having her for about four years, I got tired of hitting the ceiling every morning, awakened from a sound sleep to the head-splitting sound of absolute screaming coming from the other room. You see, these birds are a lot like roosters that crow at the crack of dawn. Being a sizable bird, about the size of a large pigeon, it had quite a set of lungs and the screaming was ear-piercing. It was kind of like hearing someone shriek who has been hit in the head with an axe. This was not my cup of tea, so I ended up giving it away to a girl who already had a cockatoo. You know, the large white birds like Baretta had on TV. I knew that she had the knowledge to take care of the bird, so I thought it would be best if Pepita and I parted ways before I served her up for an early Thanksgiving dinner. Pepita was a nice bird and I did like her but she was not my idea of a companion.

Next was the obligatory ten-gallon aquarium that I still have to this day. It is packed up neatly in the basement, eagerly awaiting the call of the fishes once again. I have had aquariums off and on since high school. Fish are fairly enjoyable, easy to take care of, and relaxing to watch, but once again not a real companion type pet. Besides, I haven't hugged a fish lately, well not the animal kind anyway, and they were a little too small to get both arms around. Plus they stink when they are out of water, so: no fish hugging.

No … a dog was the answer. Being severely allergic to cats, I could never bring myself to even think of getting one. This has been my downfall on many first dates with girls who had cats. Once I start sneezing and the eyes start watering, it's all over, much to my dating dilemma and peril. It's not that I don't like cats. They are generally pretty nice, independent, and relatively aloof which could be a problem or a blessing. Playing ball with an eager, friendly dog, whether it is big or small, is a lot more fun. With a cat you throw the ball and they lie there looking at you like "Yeah right, you expect me to get that don't you? Well, think again, captain. You can go get it yourself because I'm not moving!" Most definitely a dog was just what the doctor ordered, and how could it be anything less (or more) than a Boston terrier? Being relatively familiar with the breed from growing up with one for my first ten or eleven years on Earth, I have some of my best memories from playing with that little dog. So why not make some more new memories. For some reason, I feel that it must have been God's way of telling me that the time was right and it took the loss of my dear mother to put the wheels in motion.

CHAPTER 1

Why

Well, that was it. Mom was gone. On April 8th, 2003, a Tuesday I recall at 8:00 p.m. almost exactly, my mom passed away into the next life. She was eight days away from her seventy-eighth birthday. Having struggled for the previous couple of years with cancer on her liver, chemo treatments, and radiation therapy, it seemed to be the only release that would ease her daily pain. We were all there, my sisters Jeanne and Judy, my brother Jim, Judy's husband Ronnie and of course Dad.

We have had other relatives pass away before, grandparents, aunts, and uncles but this was a blow to our core family like no other. Death had never before touched us like this. It was a typical funeral with friends, flowers, and food. At the church service, I gave the memorial (eulogy) which was one of the hardest things I have ever done. I suppose I felt that in some way I owed it to Mom and our family to try and sum up the situation, and seventy-seven years of her life, in a satisfactory way. Leaving it to someone else to do this was not acceptable to me. I did not want anything left out and at the same time it should not drag on either. I thought that it was a little too impersonal to have a priest who really didn't know her all that well deliver the memorial. It was not hard to write but it was very difficult to deliver, in church, with everyone there who meant the most to her. I almost got through it without choking up but had to stop to compose myself just before the end. The priest who presided over the funeral told me when we were making the arrangements that it would be difficult to do, and even asked me a few times if I was sure I wanted to do it. I just couldn't see letting anyone else do it. This was probably because I felt that it was the last thing I would ever be able to do for her.

Naturally we all went through the proverbial family difficulties and the rearranging of responsibilities for a short period of time after Mom passed, but we all eventually got back to our normal routines (as if anything would ever be normal again). Normal for me, anyway, would most definitely be a new experience.

Dad started settling into a routine and generally took the bright-side approach to everything outwardly but we all knew he was struggling with his new single situation. Saying goodbye to the love of your life after fifty-nine years is probably something some of us will never have to do. It is really difficult to say how someone who has had to do this should act. I don't think that he knew what to do with himself after letting it sink in that Mom was really gone.

In any case, the days came and passed for a couple of months and during this time my sister Judy mentioned that she thought it would be a good idea if we were to buy Dad a dog – a Boston terrier. Dad used to raise Bostons years ago and she thought that it would get his mind off of everything, giving him something to do every day. I thought it was a good idea but did not think the time was right just yet. Luckily, Judy made a few calls anyway …

It was at this point that I remembered Babe, my first dog – an inherited by default Boston terrier. Being born into the family with Babe already firmly entrenched as the family pet, I had little choice. I was probably four or five years old when I first began interacting with Babe. She was a great dog who was docile, loving, and playful. I remember her being very well trained, never barked, and I do not recall her ever relieving herself in the old house on Arlington. Dad had trained her not to come out of the kitchen. The kitchen had a linoleum floor and the other rooms were carpeted so she would not come out of that kitchen for anyone except Mom and occasionally Dad. I was the newcomer as far as Babe was concerned and she accepted me as part of the family. I guess I claim her as my dog at that time because I was the youngest and everyone else was already used to her when I was born. She was a good seven years old before I was even old enough to play with her. At that time, I guess because I was a little tyke myself, I remember her being bigger than Boston terriers usually get. I have since come to realize that I was much smaller than humans get and she just *looked* bigger.

Babe was not the snarling, barking, slobbering, vicious looking bulldog or watchdog a boy of that age might like to parade around the neighborhood, striking fear into the hearts of would-be bullies and friends alike. I can attest to this fact by recalling the day I had to actually drag poor Babe out of our yard, half way down the street, after being made fun of by the older kids and trying to get her to bite them. All they had to do was yell at her before this already terrified terrier wrapped the leash around my ankles and pulled my legs right out from under me, skinning up knees, elbows, and any other fleshy part that hit the sidewalk. With me chasing after her, skinned up knees and all, she would beat a path right to our back door. Oh the humiliation for a nine year old to endure! My fierce protector was an old, nearly toothless, ugly little dog, that wouldn't even venture out of the yard, let alone "sic 'em" on command.

A few years later, Babe had to be "put to sleep" because of a series of seizures she began having at the ripe old age of thirteen. Dad said that she may have lived longer had she not run head-on smack into the hubcap on the front wheel of a moving car at our cottage at the lake. She never went out of the yard at home but at the lake we would take her on the boat with us, which meant a walk down to the water. On the way back to the cottage one day after a boat ride, she must have heard us talking or playing at the cottage and ran up the hill onto the road at the exact same time a car was passing by. She smashed right into the front left hubcap of that car. Yes, they had hubcaps in those days! Dad thought she was dead. She just lay there on the road; the car did not even know something made contact and just kept on going. Dad picked her up, sneaked her by us into the kitchen. He felt her heartbeat and could tell she was breathing. He splashed some water on her head and waved some hamburger under her nose and she woke up. She was knocked out cold by a car! She really dodged a bullet and Dad knew it. She was a tough little dog but it finally caught up with her.

One winter Monday evening a few years later I can remember lying on the floor watching *Laugh-In* (this really dates me!) when Dad came into the room and said that Babe was real sick and asked if it was OK to take her to the vet. I knew Babe was sick since I had come home from school. Neither mom nor Jeanne would let me go down the basement to see what was wrong with her. They said that she might bite me. Not really understanding that animals can get a bit *cranky* when they are sick, I was upset that they wouldn't let me see her. I was mad at both of them because I wanted to try to help her somehow. How a child my age could help is beyond me but just seeing her was the goal. I knew when Dad said that he was taking her to the vet that it was not good. What he was really saying was for my sister Jeanne and me to come and see Babe for the last time to say goodbye.

I don't recall how I felt at the time but I do remember trying to be a grown up about the whole situation. I was about ten years old and since my sister was crying, I was beginning to put the whole picture together that Babe was not coming back. Dad later told me about when he took Babe to the vet to be put to sleep. When he placed her on the floor inside the vet's operating room, the vet asked him if he wanted to stay. As Dad turned toward the vet, he saw Babe struggling to get up and come toward him to follow him. When he saw this, he couldn't take it and said "No, I'd better leave." I've thought of that often and how difficult it must have been to leave Babe behind and walk away, knowing that she wanted nothing more than to walk out with him. I still well up just thinking about that scenario and that inevitable situation that all dog owners must face, young and old alike. She lived to the ripe old age of thirteen, a good long time for a dog.

After Babe died we had a couple of other dogs, a little fuzz ball named Cocoa and a miniature poodle named Pepsi that I really didn't pay much attention to. After Babe was put to sleep, my best buddy was gone. I really did not take much of an interest in other dogs that were brought into the family. They just didn't seem to measure up to Babe. So for many years after that I just did not pay much attention to, or even think about, having a pet. I always thought that if I did have a pet I would like another Boston terrier or a bulldog but that was purely "off the cuff" thinking. I was much too busy.

For Dad in his new situation, with Mom gone and being all alone for the first time, it was a good idea to get him a little companion. Before I knew it, Judy had arranged to see a little Boston terrier breeder here in Ohio not far from Dad's house. She really hit a home run by thinking of this when she did.

Jeff Marginean

CHAPTER 2

Tiny Buttons

It was a hot August day when my sister Judy called me at work and said, "Hey, I made an appointment with the breeder to see one of the Boston terrier pups. They only have one left so we better go." A short drive into the country, which turned into a long drive trying to following my two sisters in the car ahead of me. They eventually led me to a medium-sized blue house that sat on a nice big lot.

I did not see any dogs out running around but I could hear a few barking so I assumed the dogs were kept in a pen. As we walked up the stairs to the front porch, I could feel the excitement starting to build. I was getting excited about the whole idea and I was the one who didn't think it was the right time to get Dad a dog. We entered the house and after a few polite introductions, the woman disappeared behind what I think was a dining room and was gone for a couple of minutes. When she returned, she produced the tiniest of creatures I had ever seen that was called a dog! This little thing was about the size of a gerbil and resembled some type of rodent. It was a tiny female Boston terrier that was not quite three weeks old and she was the last of the litter to be sold. She was about the size of my hand and was probably the runt of the litter. She was roughly six inches long by three inches wide with eyes that were barely open and had a little nub that was supposed to be a tail. As I stood there holding this tiny new life in my hand, the little thing started to shiver and began crawling up my arm until it could bury its little head in the crease of my inner elbow that rested against my side. With her little head buried in my side and my right hand covering her entire body, she warmed up enough to fall right to sleep.

Well, that was all it took for this hard-lined skeptic of the whole "Dog for Dad" idea to buckle under this extreme puppy pressure. We spoke with the lady for awhile about the details, such as waiting the eight weeks until the pup was on solid food, AKC registration, and other care questions. Then I asked to see the mother of this puppy. The woman left the room again and returned with a normal-sized Boston terrier with very nice markings, all black with white around the neck, white feet and white about half way up the legs. She had the trademark white stripe in the middle of her head. It was Babe! She looked just like Babe and I couldn't believe it. She was a good-looking clean dog with a sweet temperament. We left a deposit and told the woman to let us know when we could come and get the puppy. After this encounter, I was unbelievably excited about the whole idea. Even to the point of wanting my own dog again! My heart just sank to leave that little ball of fur behind. I couldn't understand it. I was supposed to be the tough guy, business minded, self-sufficient individual on the run. To feel this way, at least in recent years, was a foreign experience to me. At this point, I thought this couldn't be better for Dad, although I still didn't know how it would be received being a surprise to him.

A few weeks later, my sister called me at work and said that she had spoken to the breeder and the puppy was ready for pickup. She asked if I wanted to go and I said, "Go ahead without me and take her over. I'll stop by Dad's the next day or so." Trying to curb my enthusiasm, I forced myself not to rush right over to see our new arrival. I was excited about the new addition and really could not wait to see her but I waited until the next evening after work to stop by Dad's and say hi. Dad's house is only five minutes from my office.

When I stopped by the next day, Dad had a big smile on his face and I could see he was beaming. He absolutely loved that little dog. I said, "I hear we have a new addition!" He said, "Yeah, she is a cute little thing isn't she." As he said that, a little black and white head popped out from his sweater to see what was going on. I asked what he named her and he said "Well, when I first saw her, it looked like someone had sewed her nose on like a button, so I decided to call her Buttons." I thought, *Buttons*? And I thought Babe was a sissy name, but

11

Buttons? *Really*? She was so tiny, and after all it was a girl dog, so I thought, *OK, it seems to fit*. Like I had any say in the matter anyway. Just the same, I loved that little dog right off the bat. I mean seriously, how could anyone resist this cute little puppy? Once again I felt my self-perceived manhood taking a real beating as I recognized how I felt for this little helpless thing. I liked her even though I knew she would never be the snarling, barking, fierce attack dog that I wanted in my youth, which would love only me, of course!

Watching this playful little puppy walk around and tug on a rope made me stop and think about how completely and utterly dependent on Dad she would be. I'm sure that he knew what he was in for, although when we had puppies many years earlier, he was always working so he never had the opportunity to take care of them by himself. One of us kids would take care of them which had started way before I was even born. You can imagine the stories that this led to!

I can remember Mom mentioning it and now Dad tells the story of my sister Judy who used to put their small white Boston terrier named Beauty in a baby carriage and push her around wearing a baby bonnet. I'm not sure exactly who was wearing the bonnet but I laugh just thinking about it. She would put a bonnet on this dog and push it around the neighborhood. It wasn't like she was fifteen or anything. She was just a child at the time. That must have been a sight! Talking to Judy, she was too young to remember, probably three or four years old but I guess that little dog followed her everywhere and would even hop into the carriage whenever Judy would play with it.

I'm not even sure the name of the dog was Beauty. It could have been Spot because Dad says that it was all white except for a black spot on the back of its neck. Sounds like an inverse Boston terrier to me! Makes me wonder how much money I could make if I did that now! Put Butch in a carriage and wear a bonnet. Maybe not even at the same time. I thought about taking a picture of Butch wearing a bonnet but thought that it would be too emasculating for him and would result in years of doggie psycho-therapy just to reestablish his role as a male dog in society. Better yet, a picture of me wearing the bonnet would get more laughs and probably a lot of sympathy. I could possibly wear the bonnet while mowing my lawn. My neighbors would say, "Look at poor Jeff – the cheese has finally slid off his cracker!" Nevertheless, watching Buttons play and seeing how trusting, dependent, and affectionate she was may have stirred my protective instinct or something because in that split second my indifference toward having a dog of my own again was completely wiped away. I could see the endless hours of fun and laughing not to mention the chick magnet that dogs are! Being single, it never hurts to use all the advantages I can get!

Through the coming months, we watched Buttons grow and I was over at Dad's as much as possible. I would stop for lunch or dinner just to say hi and play with the dog. She was very feisty for a little dog and wanted to play constantly. Every time I went over there she would jump up, bark, growl, and paw at me until I would pet her. She was just the tiniest little thing – it was funny to watch her try and be ferocious. One day while we were playing on the side porch, she fell off of the carpet-covered cement step. She staggered around, and kept shaking her head like she was drunk … *Oh no!*, I thought. *I killed her!* She fell off the step and bumped her head on the cement floor. It did have a thin layer of outdoor carpet covering it but it was still cement nonetheless. It was the turf-style carpet so it was pretty thin. She fell off the step while I was playing with her so it was my fault! She whimpered, so I scooped her up and rubbed her head a little and she was just fine. She started playing within a few minutes. Whew! I told Dad to keep an eye on her because she hit her head but we have never seen anything wrong since then. Hence the saying, "Don't play on the steps!" Where have we all heard that before?

Being so active every minute of the day, Buttons wore Dad out. She wanted to play constantly and he would try to keep up to tire her out. At eighty years old, I'm sure that it was hard for him to play every time she wanted to. When it came time to have her neutered in the six month time frame, he decided that he would breed her before he got her fixed because he said it was healthier for her and he wanted to give me one of the pups for helping him since Mom had passed away. I think he saw how much I really loved Buttons and thought that I wanted one but would not ask. At that point I was hooked and really did want to have a dog but I kept saying, "I'll see when the time comes." Secretly I was glad he insisted because I couldn't wait to have one of my own.

In the spring of 2004, after Dad returned from Florida with

Buttons, he decided that he would breed her when she came into heat. He took her to our vet, Dr. Dave Soehnlen of Soehnlen's Veterinary Clinic. He had a young male Boston terrier that he wanted to breed when Dad was ready to breed Buttons. In early May, Buttons came into heat so Dad took her to be bred. It was perfect timing. The gestation period for dogs, whether large or small, is about nine weeks, so Buttons had her C-section and the new batch of pups was born on July 13th, 2004. She had five pups in her first litter. Because Boston terriers and bulldogs in general have such large heads, even as pups, it makes it difficult if not impossible for the mother to have an easy delivery on her own. This is why most vets will perform a C-section to eliminate the suffering of the birth and possible harm to the mother as well as the pups. Now, during this time the mother is naturally sedated and does not know anything that is going on and, being that this was Button's first delivery, imagine her surprise to wake up and find five strange little creatures pressing up against her! I was not there for the birth as I was once again out of town on business. Little did I realize then, that everything would change for me in the next few months.

Telling the story about when he brought the pups home, Dad recounts how Buttons ran under the bed and was terrified of them. At that point, he thought that this was going to be a big problem because it looked as if Buttons might reject them, not knowing why they are even there. After some coaxing, Buttons came out from under the bed and Dad brought the pups to her lining them up and they began to suckle. Buttons was shaking like the temperature was thirty below zero, scared to death! The nursing must have kicked in her motherly instinct because Dad said after about ten minutes of feeding, she began to clean up the puppies and groom them. From that point on, Buttons was the perfect mother, caring for and feeding them, knowing just what to do and just when to do it. She was such a sweet little dog that she never even became over-protective of the pups when we were around. After all, we were part of her family also, and were always there as far back as she could remember. What harm could we be! At the same time, we were not overly exuberant in handling the pups and Dad was just as happy to watch them fidget around in the cage except when he needed to pick them up to feed them with an eyedropper or give them some vitamins.

Even though these little balls of fur were fun to watch grow and I know Dad had fun taking care of them, they were a real handful for him. I usually went over a couple times a week to see what was going on and help when I could. With all of his experience in breeding Boston terriers, he had the matter well in hand. He even told me about how he used to feed the smaller pups with an eyedropper for the first few days if they would not eat on their own. He learned many things from his friend Sam while he bred and raised Boston terriers over fifty years ago.

As he did right from the day my sister brought Buttons home, Dad continued chiding me about picking one out. To be honest, I think I was probably more scared about the prospect of not knowing how to properly take care of him (I always knew I wanted a male) even though I secretly went and bought a couple of very good books on Boston terriers that were written by veterinarians and breeders. Reading the books it seemed a rather daunting task to take care of this animal and I was also aware of the responsibility, for possibly the next fifteen years. I told myself that, if I did choose one of these pups, I would be making a lifetime commitment and would be personally responsible for the day-to-day caring and well-being of this dog. I must have realized that this would be something like my own child and I would never give or sell this animal to anyone for any reason. Thinking of this dog as my "child" seemed really ridiculous to me at the time and I remember thinking, *I hated it when I have seen people talk to their pets like they really understand what is being said.* When I used to go to the pet store for fish or aquarium equipment, I would see people with all sorts of different dogs and I would hear grown adults say things like "Mommy and Daddy are going to feed you some good nummy nums tonight!" Then ask the question, "Would Fluffy like that?" Like the dog is really thinking in an English accent "Mmm yes mummy, nummy nums would be simply divine for this evening's dining, thank you!"

Nummy nums? You've got to be kidding me! What, exactly, is that supposed to mean? At the risk of projectile vomiting, I had to turn and walk away very quickly. I remember thinking at the time, *Oh brother, there is no way I could even* think *of saying something like that to my own kid let alone a dog.* I often thought I would try it on my fish though to see if they would understand but they were just interested in eating and swimming. They were not much for dialog and besides that I would have to yell really loud for them to hear me through the glass. Not a good policy with neighbors in close proximity who know you live alone and already think you are little nuts.

I had already been thinking about the commitment I would be making and the new enormous responsibility I would have since Dad first mentioned that he would give me a pup when he bred Buttons. I stood there staring at this writhing pile of puppies and wondered how I would ever make a choice among these five little miracles. Not taking something like this very lightly, I sat and considered the pros and cons. Should I pick one or just tell him to "sell them all?" I really couldn't resist those little helpless balls of fur and I did want one in the worst way. How would I even pick one out?

CHAPTER 3

The Chosen One

After all of the time I had progressed through various stages of life and had not given dogs much thought, I had an indescribable feeling come over me that I … well … I can't describe. It was kind of a heart-warming or maybe it was a heart-rending feeling that I had when I would see these tiny puppies. There was just something about them being so completely helpless that made me feel a little strange and I never could quite put my finger on it.

I had spent a lot of time over at Dad's house after the pups were born, watching them grow and playing with them. Most people probably already know that all they do for the first couple of weeks, or until their eyes open, is sleep, eat, and *deposit* what they've eaten all over the place. These puppies were no exception. I spent a few evenings each week after work just sitting on the floor next to them trying to decide which one, if any, I should choose for my own. I just watched them, seeing how they moved around and interacted with each other. I couldn't help but marvel at these little miracles that were twisting and squirming all over the place in front of me. Each one was different from the others even if ever so slightly. It's funny how some people would say they all looked alike and yet we could tell them apart like night and day. It must be much like parents with identical twins who know exactly which is which.

There were three males and two females. One male and one female were substantially larger than the others. All were healthy and most were pretty spunky except for the one I called Napoleon. With his white markings on his face and head, he looked like he was wearing a hat like Napoleon used to wear in the French army. Our Napoleon was the smallest pup of the litter and Dad had noticed that Buttons took extra special care of him. He was kind of a loner for the most part and over the weeks as he grew, we could see his personality start to take shape. He would play with the others for a while and then go back into the cage and fall asleep. He was very persistent when wrestling with the others and even though he was the smallest, no matter how many times he was knocked down he would get right back up and get into the fight until he was tired of it or smelled food! He was always a little different from the others and even the color of his fur was a deep wavy black like none of the others.

The others were black also but if you looked closely you could see a few brindle colored hairs in their coat. They all had very nice markings in this litter, black with white stripes on their heads all the way down to their little black noses. They had white feet and white halfway up their legs – except for the largest male. He looked like he was wearing black dress pants on his front legs with white shoes. He even had a black dot right in the middle on the top of his head in the center of the white stripe between his ears. I was told later that this is called a "Hagerty mark." The dot was supposedly named for the individual who specifically bred this into his dogs many years ago and it has since been passed down. I'm not sure if it is true or not but I don't know enough about it so I have no reason to doubt it. It was a perfect little oval shape on the top of his head. I noticed him the very first time I went to see the pups and he was the first one I ever picked up. It was very strange also that this little guy crawled up my arm and buried his head between the crease in my elbow and my side, just like Buttons did the first time that I held her. He was larger than Buttons was even at a week old. He filled my hand completely and stretched out just barely past my wrist.

The choice was simple, really. It was pretty obvious to me by now which one was right for me and I felt very lucky to have the rare opportunity at the pick of the litter. This big guy had to be my choice. He was simply too unique to let go. This was a gift from my Dad that would last the rest of my life.

All of them were cute but since I chose this one he started being cuter than the others ... and it was at this point that the "parental blindness" started to set in and I could hear something that sounded like *nummy nums* being whispered in my head. *Ahh! Oh, no! It was starting to happen.* I was transforming into a new dog dad right before my eyes.

At that point, the little guy was still very tiny and his eyes were not yet open. After choosing him out of the five pups, I made sure to go over to Dad's place a little more frequently than before and hold the little guy so that he would be used to my scent. Even before I chose this particular pup, I knew that I would name him Butch. Dad and a few other people suggested other names but no one could sway me. It was Butch or nothing.

After a couple of weeks or so, when they began to open their eyes, I was sitting in Dad's kitchen holding Butch and petting him while he slept. He was slightly outgrowing his sister who was just about the same size as him at birth. Picking him up to get a closer look at his face, I noticed something peculiar. It looked like there was something wrong with his right eye. It looked a little different than the other and my heart sank, thinking that he was blind at birth in that eye. The typical reaction of a new parent to worry about their newborn hoping that everything was all right. Taking a closer look at the eye I noticed that it was blue. *A blue eye on a Boston terrier?* I thought. *It can't be.* I have never heard of this and haven't read anything about it in the Boston terrier books that I was combing over. I said, "Dad, he has one blue eye." Dad replied, "You're kidding!" Calling him over, I headed outside to the early evening light and held him up so Dad could see and sure enough that eye was definitely blue! "I'll be, I have never seen anything like that on a Boston terrier. Can he see out of it?" "I don't know if we can tell yet," I replied. From that point, on I was always testing that eye by sneaking my finger up his right side to see if and when he would react. Worrying like a mother hen, it was all I could think about. Combing the Internet, I did find in the breed standard for Boston terriers on the AKC Web site that "Eyes blue in color or any trace of blue" were a disqualification for a show dog. Reading this did make me feel a little better, knowing that the blue eye was at least a possibility for Butch. I even caught myself praying for my new little buddy to have his sight out of that eye. For many that know me best, this reaction had they seen it would have been very foreign to them, so this is quite a confession. I think from the second that I chose Butch, my heart was immediately attached to him for life. I never really gave it much thought before but I guess it is like that for many pet owners with dogs or cats that they make a big part of their lives.

For the next few days Butch didn't seem to notice or care about me running my finger around the right side of his body. I thought, *He is blind in that eye and that's just the way it is.* Never once did the thought cross my mind that I would part with this little guy. Choosing one of the other pups over him was just not an option. I will take care of him no matter what, even though the thought of special care intimidated me even more than I was scared at the simple prospect of being responsible for another life. Butch seemed otherwise OK, growing stronger

23

and more adventurous every day. Beginning to walk around and romp with the other pups like nothing was wrong. I would get on the floor to play with all of the pups together, always separating Butch to hold him so he would know me for when the time came to take him home. Then, just when I had reserved myself to the thought of having a dog that was blind in one eye, one day I was on the floor playing with all of them and I saw Butch lying in the middle of them chewing on a toy. One of the pups was sneaking around his right side to try and steal the toy and Butch moved away from him. I thought, *He must have heard him sneaking up.* So I picked Butch up and put him in my lap, moved my finger around his right side, and he whipped his head around to see what it was! I couldn't believe it. *He can see!* I thought. I moved to another room in the house and shut the door to get away from the noise and tried it again. He reeled around when my finger was just forward of his rear leg and pounced, attacking my finger with wolf-like ferocity! (or as much wolf-like ferocity a sixteen ounce, three week old pup could muster). He really can see, and he's ferocious too! My heart leaped immediately and I had to choke back a little emotion as I realized that Butch was just fine, a perfect little pup with one blue eye! I really thought I must be nuts to have my emotions so wrapped up in this little thing that I have only known for a few weeks but I didn't care. He could see, he was healthy, and this was good enough for me. I began to see a new window of my life opening, a self-realization that I had needed to recognize for much too long a time: that there are more important things in life than getting ahead in the world.

I guess that seeing this simple animal, who knows nothing of this world, begin to see for the first time brought me back to a simpler time in my own life. It reminded me of a time when things were not so complicated. This was the first in a long line of lessons that I would be learning from Butch in the coming months and years and I was as intrigued by it as I was happy about it. Learning that there was so much more about me that I didn't know was truly a revelation. I consider myself lucky to know that I can still discover my shortcomings, work to repair them, and have the opportunity to take care of this little guy in the process.

This little being, this little life, had been placed in my care for some strange reason, but I still had to wonder whether or not I could actually take proper care of this little fellow.

CHAPTER 4

The Homecoming Dance

Anticipating the time when I would bring Butch home to stay with me, I began combing through the books which I had bought. I also searched on the Internet for how others have housed their dogs and what the breeders and veterinarians recommended. Being the type of person who takes six months to research and buy a lousy car, I just had to read absolutely everything that ever existed on the subject of owning a dog before I would feel comfortable enough to bring him home and know he would be safe.

During this time, the pups had aged to about eight or nine weeks and were weaned so Dad began to sell them off, one at a time. Each time someone came over to see them they always wanted to take Butch home with them. Dad would tell them that he was taken and they would have to choose another one. They were disappointed but the pups were all so cute it was not difficult to choose one of the others. The pups sold pretty fast with only two left, Butch and his brother Napoleon, the little one. Dad thought it would be a good idea for my brother to take Napoleon and after some thought my brother Jim decided that he would. This left Butch with Buttons, his mom, and my Dad taking care of them. Because I was not ready to take Butch home full-time at this point, Dad offered to keep him as long as I would like. This gave me the chance to take him to my house over the weekends and to gradually increase the time that I would have him there, while I figured out exactly how to take care of him.

Now, when Dad had all of the pups, they were quite mischievous as puppies can be at times and they would chew on *anything,* whether it was nailed down or not. One time, during a nice sunny late summer day, Dad took the pups outside to play. They played for awhile until they were tired out and then they went back into the house. When he made sure they were all fed and sleeping in the crate, with the door left open of course, he went to watch TV and take a nap. When he woke up after his nap he went to check on the pups and they were all gone! Including Buttons! The doors were locked, so they didn't go outside. He looked everywhere for them, under the bed, behind the cage, and behind the dresser. They were nowhere to be found. After about fifteen minutes of looking, he started hearing some faint squealing coming from the headboard of the bed. Kneeling down and taking a closer look under the bed, he saw some lumps moving around *inside the boxspring*! Those little rascals, namely Buttons, had chewed a hole through the material underneath the boxspring at the foot of the bed. Then they all crawled in and went to the head of the bed, inside the boxspring, where they huddled up and went to sleep. The only way Dad could get them out was to slice open the bottom of the boxspring and pull them out one by one. From that point on, and one queen-sized boxspring later, it remained a point of contention because the dogs always wanted to get in there and it was the first place Dad looked when he could not find them. It seemed, at first, that Butch was the ringleader in this caper but after watching them one day, we realized that it was Cindy, Butch's sister, who was the perpetrator. The rest were merely following her to the head of the boxspring and then Butch would push his way past the rest to be in the front. Terrific! That's one more thing to add to the list to puppy-proof my house. I was sure Butch would be doing this while he was still small enough.

I have to say, and even Dad admits, that even though they were a lot of work for an eighty year-old man, they sure were a lot of fun for him to watch, all of them playing with each other and sleeping in a little pile. They filled his days nicely with their constant need for attention.

I'm not really the picture-taking type, spending long hours poring over old pictures or planning to take new ones, but I do like staying up-to-date with the current technology. Seeing that these pups were growing fast and that this was a unique time of our lives, I purchased a good digital camera to capture the moments. Now I'm glad I did because someday I'll be able to look back at this and remember the fun Dad and I had with them.

Naturally, as the pups began to get stronger, they would find plenty of mischief to get into and Butch was no exception. Only a few weeks old and those little dogs were scurrying around and running up and down the hall as fast as they could. Living in my house by myself, and keeping things relatively orderly, I knew that I was going to need to really make an effort to outsmart Butch and head off possible chewing problems and other hazards before we did the whole "homecoming dance." At first I put his cage in my bedroom and locked him in there overnight just so he would not roam the house and hurt himself while I was asleep. This went on for about six or eight months. Then I would just leave his cage door open at night and he would go in there when he was tired and stay there on his own. Having an extra bedroom in the house, I thought I would fix it up so he could stay in there during the day when I was not home. It had a brand new mattress and boxspring along with the usual bedding, which was also new. Becoming the new "dog dad" and the "puppy-proofing engineer" that the job called for, I began to devise my plan for his room. I would make it indestructible ... so I thought!

Using three sheets of four inch by eight inch plywood, I made a surround for the entire bed. It was about thirty-six inches high on three sides with the fourth side being the wall at the headboard. This was so designed that we would not have any of those boxspring episodes that Butch was used to at Dad's house. The floor was covered in older carpet and the bedroom set was the one I've had since high school so I was not too concerned about it being chewed on. This was "Butch's room" and any time someone would come over to my house I pointed it out to them as such and usually got a funny reaction. "Butch's Room?" they would say, raising an eyebrow. "You mean he has his own room?" I would say "Yeah, why not? I have the extra room and he seems to like it in there when I'm gone." I guess they thought it strange that this little ten-pound animal had his own room but neither Butch nor I thought that there was anything out of the ordinary.

Once he was a little older, he would stay in *his* room while I was gone for a few hours at a time, so he would not hurt himself running around the house, chewing on wires, or more expensive furniture. Some people would say that I could just leave him in his cage while I was gone but I couldn't see myself doing that. The room was plenty big enough where he could run around a bit and play with some toys I would leave in there for him. Going against the advice of the veterinarian books that I had read, I left some water and some dry food in there in case he got hungry. In general, it was a safe, secure, nice sized room for a small dog who couldn't possibly get into any trouble in there and would only chew on the toys I gave him and run and frolic in his room while I was away. *Yeah right!* I'm not exactly sure what dimension I was living in to think up this perfect-puppy scenario but now let me tell you the graphic details.

31

The long and short of it is don't expect to get a puppy of *any* breed and think you are going to get away without the odd torn carpet, couch, or furniture. Even the occasional hole in the wall is not out of the question.

I had to be willing to accept a certain amount of damage and not regret having Butch or taking it out on him. Dogs generally can't help it in many cases and in many other cases it's more the owner's fault than it is the dog's. I had to constantly be thinking about what he would be doing while I was away and not put him in a position where he would have an opportunity to wreak havoc on a piece of property that I cared about. I was at least smart enough to know that if you come home hollering at the pup every day for doing something bad it will become a routine and then it could develop other bad habits purely out of fright. When a puppy associates your coming home every day with your hollering at him, well it can lead to other destructive and messy habits associated with stress and anxiety.

He is just like a little kid and although he lives to please me, he also has his own attitude and thoughts. Yes, I said thoughts! Sometimes I can just look at Butch and imagine what he is thinking. He has his "tired" look, his "excited" look, and his "curious" look. I was so surprised at how smart he was that I really expected him to start talking any day. So while thinking about how I could keep that room puppy-proof, I also had to keep in mind how fast he was learning to get around my daily remedies to his devious antics. The trick was not to be too obvious and also make the room as comfortable as possible for him.

For the first couple of weeks that Butch was in his room for a few hours at a time it went pretty well. He didn't relieve himself in there at all and I could see where he had been playing with his toys and chewing nicely on the items that I left for him. I also kept a nice little clock radio in there to play some soft music and keep him company. One day I thought it would be a good idea to get him a little stuffed-animal dog with a squeaker and leave it with him so he would have a buddy. This stuffed animal was as big as he was and seemed to be made pretty well. After all, I did buy it at a pet store so it must be OK for him, right? I came back an hour later and I heard this steady "squeak," "squeak," "squeak" coming from the room. I thought, *That's great he likes his new buddy.* But you can guess what I found. I opened the door and it was snowing in that room. One million little white hair clumps over every square inch of carpet. He ripped the stuffing out of that thing and shredded the casing into nice long thin strips with the occasional slobber-coated balled-up piece. He was just lying on the floor chomping on the squeaker that was inside the now molecule-sized stuffed dog. He looked at me as if to say, "Oh, you're home. I believe I will now retire into the den." He stood up and walked right past me. I said "Hey, where do you think you are going?" He stopped only long enough to turn his little head back around to look at me, probably thinking, *Be sure to have that mess cleaned up by the time I go in there again!* It wasn't until the next day that I understood the real meaning of love and being a new dog dad.

The next day was Saturday and as was the routine, Butch would bang on his crate door to wake me up so I could let him out. When I let him outside to relieve himself, he came back and was limping very badly with his hind-end almost dragging on the ground. It was then that I noticed something trailing behind him. A closer look revealed that it was not only trailing behind him but was still attached to his innards. This was no doubt a nice long remnant of his buddy that he had shredded and eaten the day before. Well, my new dog-dad superpowers kicked in and I quickly surmised that I would have to take the matter into my own hands and remove the obstruction. It was a brilliant deduction on my part. I grabbed a paper towel and delicately completed the function. When I put Butch down, he was so happy that he playfully grabbed my ankle and ripped the sock I had on, completely oblivious to what just happened. Ah, I was a new dog dad at long last!

Keeping an eye on what he was chewing in the way of furniture and other non-digestible items would be paramount for the next couple of years. Learning my lesson from the stuffed animal, I bought more than a couple of other rubber toys from the cheap plastic to the expensive thick rubber. They must have thought I was nuts at the pet store, walking to the checkout with nearly one of every type of chew-toy or rawhide they had. Surely, with this many toys, he would find something he liked that he could not destroy!

A few weeks passed and Butch was doing really well, playing with the toys I left for him while I was gone. He still wasn't relieving himself in his room or in the house. I made sure not to leave him alone for too long and that someone was available to let him out if I could not be there. Then, one day, I came home from work and I could hear him scrambling around behind the door. He knew I was home and was getting excited to see me. What a great feeling to have someone there to come home to. I tried to open the door and I could feel a strange resistance. The door only opened a couple of inches and I could see Butch's little nose poking through the crack with his tongue going a mile a minute but I couldn't open the door more than a couple of inches. After I realized that he was not hurt it began to sink in that the carpet was blocking the door. How on earth could … the … carpet … be …

After I was able to force the door open and peek inside, Butch came running out and started jumping on me while tugging on my socks. I pushed my head in the door and saw that the carpet had been literally ripped in half from one end of the room nearly to the other. I stood there absolutely dumbfounded, staring at millions of chewed bits of orange padding and a six by ten foot piece of carpet that used to cover half the floor. All I could do was stand there and wonder how long it took him to tear the carpet to that extent. I thought about getting mad for a minute and I did holler at him a little but in all fairness to him, the carpet already had a small tear that he apparently found during his daily exploits in his room. I could hardly stay mad at him because it was my fault for not thinking that he would find that small tear and go to work on it. The carpet was already badly worn so it was not really a big loss.

Two separate issues arose from that incident. The first was

starting to price hardwood flooring and the second was learning of his affinity for carpet padding. To think that I could put two and two together and recognize that he was going after the padding instead of the carpet would be giving me way too much credit. This can be demonstrated by the small dug-out holes in corners of nearly every room in my house over the next year! I thought I was going to have to have cement floors before he would stop digging them up. It was at the point where he was about five months old, during the winter, that I started to realize that his shortcomings and incidents of apparent disobedience were my failings. I began to learn the importance of not setting him up for failure by not thinking like a puppy. I had to learn to think ahead of him about what he would be trying to chew next rather than giving him more responsibility than he can handle.

Having no kids of my own (yet!), I can imagine that this philosophy is used by many new parents. It gave me a whole new respect for single parents and what they go through raising a child. Eventually, the child grows up. Dogs, generally speaking, age physically but in most cases stay a puppy at heart, playing throughout their lives. I suppose humans are to blame for this, if blame is actually necessary, although I don't know anyone who has a dog that doesn't like to come home to the daily unfailing "Glad to see you!" excitement.

House training was another issue that I was concerned about before I decided to accept Butch into my life. I thought that I was getting into months on end of rigorous twenty-four fun-filled hours a day house training Butch. I later realized that thinking he had excrement shooting from his behind and ears all day and night was slightly ridiculous. Reading the books on behavior, using my own common sense, and just getting to know him were the best ways to show him where and when to go. Surprisingly, Butch would wake me up in the morning when he had to go outside by banging on his cage door just before the alarm clock went off. This training chore proved to be much easier than I thought. I did not understand that, when left with a choice, dogs will not "lay an egg" in the area where they sleep or play unless it is an accident. I made sure to play with Butch in every room of the house and to go in and out of them pretty frequently so he would attribute the whole house as at least a playground. This was not hard to do because my well-hidden, never-ending, childlike attitude rears its head occasionally and I was only too happy to share it with Butch.

Running through the house, chasing miniature footballs from room to room, and throwing toys the length of the house was a daily occurrence when we were not outside playing. Not to mention the obligatory tug of war with the small rope or knotted up socks. (Now I know why he always chews at the socks I'm wearing!) Obviously I live alone because a female in the house would be on pins and needles as I threw the ball just inches from wall sconces and pictures, then went rambling, with Butch, around the furniture to get to it first while "gently" knocking delicate items off the surrounding tables! I'm quite sure the neighbors heard us running around in the house but I'm also sure that they were used to the strange noises emanating from my house after all of these years and just considered this latest commotion as normal. They know me well enough to come right out and ask what all the racket was about last night!

After all the years of work and little or no play at all, I was turning into what I would often criticize, if not out loud at least to myself: someone who didn't care about getting ahead in life. Mistakenly, I felt that I should always be working or thinking about work in some form or another, not taking the time to "smell the roses." Unknowingly, with all his little quirks, with all of his chewing things up, and the occasional accident in the house, my new little companion was turning into "my little buddy." He was awakening a part of me that I had forcibly subdued and long forgotten. I didn't know I had it in me any longer to care this much for something so tiny and simple, allowing myself the forbidden luxury of thinking of something other than work.

CHAPTER 5

The Terminator Puppy

Not knowing much about taking care of a puppy when I brought Butch home for the first time, I was consumed with reading everything I could find on the subject as to not make any obvious mistakes while learning to care for him. Naturally I narrowed my research to Boston terriers because they do have some very breed-specific characteristics that need special consideration. Their "pushed-in face" and their flat muzzle tend to make this bulldog-like creature have trouble breathing. In addition, they cannot tolerate extreme heat or cold very well, so you really have to be careful with them when going outside. I guess, being the new dog dad, I tended to err on the side of caution even if it did curtail our fun every now and then. On the positive side, these dogs shed very little if at all and they are generally very clean as house dogs go, so you don't have to give them too many baths throughout the year. If you feed them a good premium dog food and rub them down three or four times each week, their coat will stay shiny and clean and you won't find little hairs all over the house. I also read a few books on training dogs in general to see how Butch would stack up and to see if I could actually teach him tricks that other dogs could do. Taking in as much information as I could, I started to understand that the conflicting information I was reading was based on (1) the experiences of the people writing it and (2) the fact that the personalities of these dogs can be very different. I decided that too much information could be a bad thing because it starts to get confusing, and then you spend most of your time worrying. I shelved the books, threw caution to the wind, and started taking it a day at a time.

It became a ritual for me to get on the floor and play with Butch every night, throwing the ball, tugging on rope, and carefully wrestling around with him. He was a fast learner and after I would hide the ball from him a couple of times, he would be on to me and knew exactly where to find it. At this point I still didn't know the extent of his learning capability nor did I understand how smart dogs can be. I had read that the Boston terrier breed was extremely intelligent but I had no relative experience to gauge it on and just chalked it up to someone being partial to the breed.

Now all along I had been trying to teach him the basics that I read about in the books. You know, "sit," "stay," and "down," to get him to lay on the floor and he was picking them up quickly. Then, one day, we were playing with the ball on the floor. I was throwing it back into the kitchen and he would run as fast as he could to get it and bring it back to me. It started to get kind of monotonous, probably more for me than him because he would chase the ball one hundred times if I threw it, so I thought I would try to change the game a bit. I made him lay on the floor in front of me then I would slowly place the ball on the floor in front of him. After one or two times of him pouncing on my hand with the ball, I made him stay while he was lying on the floor and I placed the ball on the floor again slowly pulling my hand away. It was comical to watch him tremble, wanting to jump on that ball and twitch with every small move I made but he stayed there and learned, after a few tries, not to jump on it until I said "OK." It was a race to the ball. I would increase the distance to the ball each time and we would both try to get it before the other. After a couple of evenings of this, we were playing again and I was just tossing the ball behind me while watching TV. Butch would run and get the ball and place it in my hand so I could try to get it from him. He would *never* let that ball go without a tug of war. I threw the ball a few times, and once, when he returned with the ball I couldn't believe my eyes. He dropped the ball in front of me, backed up a few steps, laid down in front of it and looked at me. When I moved to pick up the ball he pounced on it before I could get it. *He was actually playing the game I had taught him*! I could not believe my eyes. *There is no way that this little dog could learn that so quickly,* I thought. I tested this theory a few more times and I was astounded that he could repeat it over and over again at his will. Realizing that Butch was smarter than I gave him credit for, I knew I would have to try to think up new ways to keep him occupied and to stimulate his brain. This would prove to be quite a challenge. Trying to differentiate between his instinct and his learning capability would be my first test.

Although he was only four or five months old, he was pretty quick afoot. Still being just a pup, he had really sharp teeth and nails and was not afraid to use them. Needless to say, my hands and forearms were scratched up a good bit but he couldn't help it and he wasn't doing it on purpose. He seemed to like to play kind of rough and tumble but I was careful not to pull back on anything he was holding in his mouth, just allowing him to tug on it. I would never manhandle him either. He was still a little pup and we were both learning how to play together. Since it was still fall in Ohio, we were treated to the occasional nice warm day so we would be outside running around chasing the ball around the yard. This was also about the time I started throwing the Frisbee® for him, even though it was as big as he was and he had to more or less drag it back to me rather than carry it.

Living in a small city not far from a golf course, there were plenty of rabbits, squirrels, skunks, opossum, and groundhogs wandering around. With these benign ground creatures come the inevitable predators such as owls, hawks, and the occasional fox that I had to watch out for, not to mention the domestic cats that made my yard part of their nightly rounds. Even though by now he was growing fast and weighed about eight or nine pounds, my 150 foot square corner lot was quite a big jungle for such a little pup. It was up to me to keep an eye open for potential danger. Butch had plenty of space to run, shrubs to explore, and many possible new friends to meet, as their owners would walk their dogs past my house. Butch took an early interest in the shed, which had been home to a growing family of rabbits for the last few years. Knowing that I could not use any weed killer on the lawn because of the possible ill effects it could have on Butch's health, there was quite a cornucopia of delectable offerings for these vegetarians growing in my yard. This, along with plenty of cover, made it perfect for a young rabbit family to get a good start in the world. Little did I know that Butch would find this to his liking. Now, I know that a wolf's instinct includes hunting, and that all dogs are descended from wolves, but Butch was a just young terrier so I never imagined what I would witness with my own two eyes!

On one of the nice warm fall Saturdays, I was in my garage working with the door open and Butch was sitting at the entrance watching me. Just when I turned to see what he was doing, a little rabbit hopped around the corner not two feet from where Butch was sitting. Before I knew what had happened, Butch took off running after that surprised rabbit and after about ten yards all eight pounds of him pounced on a rabbit that was barely smaller than him. Obviously, it was a young rabbit but nonetheless this was quite a feat for a young dog of any breed. I ran over to the two of them while they were struggling. Butch had the matter well in hand, or should I say in teeth, with his mouth around the rabbit's neck. I grabbed Butch, pulled his jaws apart, and let the rabbit loose. I watched him scurry off into the backyard and Butch actually took off after him again! This time the rabbit had put enough ground between them to make it under the shed before Butch could grab him again. Butch almost followed it under the shed but he was not quite small enough to squeeze his body through the opening between the floor of the shed and the ground. He frantically paced around sniffing and trying to find a way in, scratching at the ground and the bottom of the wooden shed. By the time I arrived on the scene from across the yard, Butch was digging a full-blown tunnel, widening the entrance where the rabbit went in. I grabbed him and carried him back to the house and he looked at me like I just killed his mother. After seeing his blue eye turn red in the pictures I had been taking, and witnessing this latest display, I thought to myself, *I have a real life "Terminator Puppy" on my hands!*

Thinking about this unusual behavior for a while, I came to more than one conclusion about the outdoor habitat – a habitat over which Butch had apparently elected himself military dictator. First of all, I was going to have to respect his speed. Small to midsize dogs of most breeds, especially terriers of all types, are so-called "ratters," which generally means they were bred to hunt small prey of any kind. I now knew that I was going to have to find a foolproof way to rein him in so that he did not go running into the street. Living on a corner of two streets made it especially important to prevent him from chasing or following any small game onto either street and ending up "road pizza" if he decided to hunt in a neighbor's yard. Second,

I was going to have to train him to recognize the boundary of his new "country," the country that he was now brutally seizing from the current residents while installing himself as the new military dictator. Third, I was going to have to be careful to watch what he was up to when we were outside, while he was still a pup, as it was not unusual for the odd skunk or opossum to wander right into the garage looking for a quick snack of grass seed or anything else they might want to eat.

This fact was demonstrated to me a few years ago before I even had Butch. I had been an avid weekend golfer, golfing every Saturday morning, if the weather permitted, from early April to late October. In the summer months, I still spend much time in the garage, which is attached to the house, reading the paper or fiddling around with some kind of outdoor project. It is a two-car garage so it has plenty of space to move around. This means that the garage door is often open late into the night before I go to bed. Sometimes even after midnight. Well, one summer Friday night as I was going to bed, I decided to put my clubs in the truck and get ready for golf the next day. So I proceeded into the garage and as I was putting the clubs in the truck I smelled that familiar skunk smell that we all know and love. This was not unusual, as every so often one of the neighbor's night-stalking cats may have run into one, got into a scrape, and was sprayed by the skunk, dragging the smell throughout the neighborhood. I would also see a skunk from time to time as I was driving home from a late night excursion, so it was nothing new. Not thinking anything of it I went back inside, closed the garage door, which has an automatic garage door opener, closed the windows, and turned on the air conditioning for the night. Up bright and early the next day I made my coffee, dressed for golf, and was on my way. About five hours later I returned home and as I pulled into the garage I noticed what I thought was a plastic grocery bag rippling just inside the garage near the right side rail that the door travels on. I pulled in, got out of the truck, walked around the back end of the truck, and as I came closer to the "grocery bag" it quickly became clear that this was no grocery bag. I heard the scratching and saw the twitching tail very plainly at this point. *It was a skunk, and it was alive in my garage*!

Although I didn't scream like a little sissy, I can say that I did jump out of my skin when this realization hit me. After pondering this situation for a few minutes, I put my skin back on and went into the house, trying to figure out what I was going to do about this peculiar situation. I went back outside into the garage to get a better look, being careful just in case he aimed his little butt at me. He was not hissing or snorting but he was most definitely stuck somehow by what appeared to be his head. I went back in to get my binoculars and get a good close up look at the little guy and sure enough his head was stuck between the rail of the garage door and the wood frame at the lowest bracket. Looking around the garage doing a bit of detective work, I noticed that the bag of grass seed had been punctured at the bottom and some of the seed was scattered over the floor around it. I must have closed him in the garage late the previous night and he was hiding when I loaded up the truck. He must have been closed in the garage all night and got stuck looking for a way to get out. Otherwise, he would have run out when I opened the door to leave in the morning. Looking closer at the door, I could see that the rail and the frame was in a slight V shape and his head was resting on the lower bracket holding the rail to the frame. He must have stood on his hind legs and sniffed the air coming through the crack of the door with his head between the rail and the frame while sliding down to find an opening to get out, then tried to pull his head out without sliding back up to the wider portion where he stuck it through. When he realized he was stuck, he probably panicked and sprayed a little, creating the fabulous aroma which filled the garage. The funny thing was that his head was stuck just high enough that his butt was firmly on the ground, as though he was just sitting there, so spraying me or anyone else was out of the question. OK, great, so now I know how he got there but just what, exactly, was I going to do about getting him out of there?

I thought I would back the truck up against that side of the garage and stand on the tailgate while I wedged a board between the rail and the frame to widen it enough for him to pull his head out. With me standing on the bed of the truck, I would be high enough that he would not see me and could run away. Then I thought that he might be hurt and would just get hit by a car and die. Besides that, his head was too close to the bracket connecting the rail to the frame for me to widen it out enough anyway. Nuts! Now what? I did not have a clue what to do at this point. I knew that I could kill it very easily with a hammer and it would only take one stroke. He would feel no pain. I could let it stay there for a week or two and starve to death. There were many reasons that I chose not to do either of these things like not wanting to smell skunk in my garage, not to mention my house, for the next year but most of all I did not want to hurt the little guy. It wasn't his fault; he didn't know any better. He was not squirming or even panicking when I came near him but he was squeaking a little. After about an hour of jockeying around for something to do, I decided I would call the police. I'll never know where this thought came from but I didn't know what to do at this point so I thought I would let them in on my predicament.

I live in a small city, not *Mayberry* small, but small by big city standards. We have a great police department and they do a great job of keeping the city safe. I'm sure they get many strange calls but the laughter that I heard on the other end of the line was a little more than what I had expected. After I explained what had happened, the responses I got made me laugh just as hard. I heard things like "What do you want us to do? Get some little hand cuffs and leg irons and bring him downtown for questioning?" and "Do you want to press charges? Should we arrest him for breaking and entering? Or how about theft, maybe we could make that stick for stealing grass seed, how much did he take? A paper cup full?" "BAAA HAAA HAA!" It was like I was watching a sit-com on TV. Realizing that I was getting nowhere, I told them if anyone had any ideas to give me a call. Just when I thought that I was out of options the phone rang. It was one of the police officers who had just returned to the station calling me back. He said, "You won't believe this, but I just left a wildlife trapper up at the high school. He comes to town about once a month to trap groundhogs and rodents that dig up the ball fields and the stadium field at the high school." Since I live about a half a mile from the school this was perfect. He said, "I'll go back and tell him to come down to your house before he leaves." I thought, *Wow, this is great.* Just when I thought the conversation was over, the officer said, "I'll come down also so I can ask that skunk a few questions, HAAA HAAA! See you in about thirty minutes!" I suppose I deserved that but it was really a stroke of luck and the police did come through for me.

About a half hour later, the trapper showed up. He was a nice guy and he introduced himself as Paul from All Creatures Big and Small. They are a humane wildlife and insect control company. " I was told by the police that you had a bit of a problem and wanted me to stop by," Paul said. I answered him, "Yep, you could call it that," as I pointed to the corner of the garage. When he walked up into the sight line of the skunk, that little skunk started hissing and throwing a fit! He asked, "Wow! Was that guy hissing like that all this time when he saw you?" I said, "No, not at all, just a whimper now and then." He said, "He knows you then." I replied "I've never seen a skunk around my house here before." Paul said, "I'm sure you have smelled him though, since he didn't hiss at you, he definitely knows you. He must have been coming around for awhile and your house is on his regular route. I've seen a few strange things before but this ranks right up there as pretty bizarre!"

I told him that I didn't want to hurt the little guy so he gave him an injection and just knocked him out so he could take him back out into the country and release him with the groundhogs that he had trapped at the school. While the skunk was knocked out, I loosened the bolts on the bracket and Paul pulled him out and inspected his neck. He looked to be fine. No bleeding or anything, just a little fur scraped off. After we inspected him for injuries, Paul put him in a cage and loaded him in his truck, "I've only got about thirty minutes before he wakes up so I better get out of here." He then produced a small spray bottle and went to the corner of the garage where the skunk was and sprayed the floor. Imagine my surprise when the skunk odor completely went away. "What is that stuff? It's great!" I asked. He said, "It's a secret concoction that neutralizes the odor. It works pretty well for me." I was never able to get it out of him, but I knew that this guy really knew his stuff after that and was just glad he was available. He only charged me sixty bucks for his time and the shot and he was on his way. I would gladly have paid more but he said that it was a fair price. Whew! What an ordeal.

Recalling this situation and not wanting to deal with a skunk-smelling Butch, I had to redefine my attitude when working around the yard, knowing that Butch was capable of such ferocious behavior in wanting to exact the death penalty for any interlopers coming into the yard. Still being a pup, I'm sure a nice-sized opossum, groundhog, or a larger adult cat could really inflict some damage to Butch, if not kill him, if they were to tangle. I'm also sure that the hawk or the owl probably had their eye on him once or twice as a large tasty morsel, so Butch's outdoor safety was number one on the list at least until he was a little bigger. It wasn't long before he was big enough to handle himself out in his wild new territory.

CHAPTER 6

Doctor, Doctor

From the time Butch was very small until he was about three years old, I had quite a hard time relating any potential problems that he may be having to his vet Dave Soehnlen of Soehnlen Veterinary Clinic. Dave came very highly recommended from the breeder where we bought Buttons and he has been around for quite awhile. I later came to learn that his family and my brother-in-law's family all grew up together which made me feel more comfortable taking Butch to him. He has an affinity for Boston terriers and has had a number of them as pets throughout the years. He has a very nice clinic located on a farm where he cares for all sorts of animals, large and small, but it was his years of knowledge and experience with the Boston terrier that kept me going back to him for help and regular checkups for Butch. There were many times I would ask a pretty stupid question and he would patiently answer, giving me all of the information that he could think of on the topic I brought up. Trying to study every dog ailment known to man, I would even look up Butch's symptoms on the internet. This may not have been the best idea because, on more than one occasion, I would read about some debilitating dog problem and look at Butch and say, "Oh no, he has *trickstadecaphobia* with a *rhinitis* that I just read about that dogs sometimes get and he is going to die in five minutes!" This example might seem absurd but it was close to my way of thinking at the time.

It wasn't quite as bad as that but there was the time I took Butch into the vet because he just wasn't his same old spunky, jumping-around self. This happened when he was about two years old. He looked kind of down and dragged out so I could tell he was not feeling good. This was a first for him – and for me – because he was always in good health, even in the winter time. When he started to shiver, I thought that he was really getting sick with a fever. Years ago when I was pretty young, when I would get a fever, Mom could always tell because I would get what she called the "chills." Having a fever is usually how I started to shiver when I was getting sick. Putting two and eight together: shivering = chills, chills = fever, fever = Butch is sick. In this way, I deduced that he had a dog flu of some kind and I should take him to the vet as soon as possible.

Arriving at the vet, I carried him in and Dave saw him right away. Butch was really shivering but at this point I'm sure that the increase was because he hates going to the vet anyway and it usually means some sort of uncomfortable anal probing or the like, but I'll get to that later. He knows the building and seemingly knows the route or the timing. If we are in the truck just a little longer than it takes to get to my Dad's house, he knows something is up and he can pretty well guess what is in his immediate future. He is probably thinking, *Oh no, we're going to the hall of torture again!* It's kind of how I feel going to the dentist. He really does not like being at the vet. I felt bad for him because I have learned that Butch will shiver when he is cold (duh!), sick, or scared. It's his natural reaction to these things in most cases. Traveling on that train of thought a little further led me to reason that since Butch was so young and had not yet experienced many things, like being sick, that he could potentially be scared because he didn't know what was happening or why he was feeling so bad.

So as we are all standing there, Dave, an assistant, and me, he asks, "What seems to be the problem?" He starts running his hands over Butch and looking into his eyes and ears searching for some outward sign of a problem. "He's sick. He just has not been himself for the last couple of days and he has not been eating," I replied. As they moved Butch around to take his temperature, with a rectal thermometer of course, I mentioned "He has been shivering and I think he has the chills." They said "The chills?" followed by a hearty chuckle from everyone in the room. "Yes," I said, "You know like when you have a fever, you get the chills!" I think they thought that I was kidding but being the dog novice that I am I did not know any other way to describe it. At first I thought that they might think I meant "chillin'" like relaxing or something. It's not uncommon for them to get a kick out of my interpretations of Butch's perceived ailments.

After a couple minutes passed Dave pulled the thermometer out and said "Hmmm, his temperature is up slightly. It's 102. OK for cats but a little high for dogs. So he definitely has some sort of bug." He asked, "Do you know if he has eaten anything weird lately?" I said, "He is always rooting around in the yard and I know that there is owl droppings on my sidewalk that he always sniffs around – he did kill another squirrel a few days ago but he didn't eat any of it." He said it was probably a virus of some kind and explained that in some cases it is best just to let them work it out on their own and for me to monitor if it got any worse or if he continued not eating. He went on to say that dogs are just like us in some ways. He may just not feel good and is having a bad couple of days. He did not want me to let it go if Butch did not improve in a day or two but he did not want to jump into diagnosing anything until Butch had some time to work it out on his own. Luckily, Butch improved the very next day which was probably not luck, it was probably just normal.

It was at this point that I invoked the two- or-three-day rule for similar situations. If and when Butch wasn't quite feeling good and I could visibly tell, I would try to make him take it easy and keep a close eye on him. If he did not improve in two days, I would call the vet and take him in on the third. Obviously, if there was some outward ailment that I knew was going to develop into a problem I would call right away. But for just run of the mill not feeling well, I would wait it out.

This new philosophy came in quite handy one day when I all of a sudden noticed that Butch had a large red patch protruding from under his blue eye. I thought it was peculiar and it just happened overnight. A closer look revealed that was his third eyelid swelling up for some reason. With my quick canine medical intellect and reflexes, I dashed to the computer with lightning speed to look up dog eye ailments on the internet. (Yes, you know what's coming. Here we go again!) It's a good thing that I did because I found out that Butch had conjunctivitis. *This is terrible, now what do I do?* I thought. Off to the phone! I dialed the phone to call the vet, pressing the numbers with superhero-like accuracy. I explained that I needed to talk to Dave because I thought Butch had conjunctivitis. "Dave, I think Butch has conjunctivitis because his third eyelid is swelling from the bottom of his blue eye," I declared confidently. Dave replied, "How long have you noticed this?" I said, "Just today." He then asked, "What dog book are you reading now and where have you taken Butch over the last couple of days?" Well, this prompted a bit of a chuckle and then I began to recount how Butch and I went for a walk through the field of a new development going in close by my house. We walked for a good hour through tall weeds and brush. "He probably has an allergy to something you ran across in the field. He sniffed it up and is probably having a reaction. Wait a couple more days and bring him in if it doesn't get better." Dave advised. Well, it did get a little worse before it got better. The next day both eyelids were a little swollen. I took him over to Dad's and he took a look at Butch and said the same thing Dave did, "He's probably allergic to something. Just leave him alone a couple of days." The third day showed a remarkable improvement with barely any swelling at all and only in one eye. Once again, the three-day rule applied. I should have listened to myself. I'm sure experienced mothers and fathers would get a good laugh at this reaction of mine, but they may understand my worry. Maybe I'm being trained for the real thing some day!

All of this pseudo knowledge from someone that didn't even know what a flea looked like. I recall the first time I took Butch to the vet with Dad and Buttons. I had been wondering why Butch was scratching himself and was afraid that he might have fleas. Being such a novice, and taking the same methodical, slow approach to learning every facet of Butch's daily life, it never occurred to me that he just might have an itch that he needed to scratch. If I was wearing a fur tuxedo all day I suppose I would have a few itches that needed scratched also!

So there we are. Dave, Dad, Butch, and me as Dave starts to look him over. I said, "He seems to scratch a lot and I wasn't sure if he had fleas." He asked, "Have you seen any?" I replied, "I don't think so. I don't even know what they look like. I'm not sure I'd know one if I had seen one. The only ones I have seen were cartoons and six feet tall!" They looked at me as if I had monkeys flying out of my ears. Dad chimed in "Are you serious? You don't know what a flea looks like?" I said, "No, I've never had them. What do they look like?" He proceeded to grab a piece of paper and pencil and draw a flea. He said, "Here, this is what they look like." "That's just a black dot," I said. Dave turned and said, "Well, that's what they look like, a little dark oval that scurries out of the light and Butch doesn't have fleas." He continued, "He just has an itch that needed scratching. Just like us, they have to scratch sometimes too!" After another good laugh, they then showed me how to search around on Butch for fleas. Under his legs, where there is bare skin and his fur starts, is a likely place to find them and also around his ears and under his tail. One more learning experience but it wasn't even the highlight of the visit.

It was at this point where the entire experience of owning a dog took a most unpleasant and unexpected turn. You see, I also had noticed that Butch had started to scoot across the floor a few days earlier and this is what prompted me to think that he may have fleas. Imagine my surprise when Dave asked most specifically if I noticed if Butch was scooting across the floor at any time recently. Scooting, as you may know, is when the dog sits his hind end on the ground and pulls himself across the floor with his front paws. I had not yet reached this point in the veterinary books that I was reading. Dave began to explain the reason for this scooting or "butt scratching" activity that dogs sometimes undertake, "He needs to have his anal sacks expressed." "Anal sacks expressed? I think he expresses his anal sacks just fine, often in the middle of the night usually right in my face." Dave chuckled and said, "No, no, no, Butch, and most dogs, have anal scent sacks that they use to mark when they expel waste. Somewhere along the way in domestic

59

dogs these sacks started to not get used as much as they should. These sacks can fill up and sometimes get infected if they are not emptied out regularly. You can usually tell when they are bothering them if they start to scoot around on their behind." "Oh terrific!" I said. "Now how am I supposed to do that?" I watched Dave get a surgical glove, squeeze some gelatinous glob on his index finger and he said, "Please hold him still." He then slowly poked his finger into Butch's rear and his little bulbous eye bulged out a little more than I thought they could. Dave said, "Yep, they are pretty full." He then gave a quick squeeze and Butch let out a yelp. Dave took a quick look at what came out and said it's OK. "It's all normal stuff coming out. If it was infected it would be more of a paste."

Oh yummy! This is just great, this top secret information that has been withheld from me since I was a child is now at the forefront of my neurotic dog parenting journey. Why didn't anyone tell me about this? I was now afraid that I would have some sort of fixation on Butch's anal gland problems, along with everything else. I mean, I have nothing against a good anal gland expressing every now and then, especially after a good Mexican dinner, but this activity was a little more than I am capable of in Butch's case. I think my biggest fear is that I would hurt him in some way, not knowing what I am doing. I think that this area is better left to a professional.

Although he did not have an infection, he was decidedly more bouncy and lighter on his feet. There must be something to this anal gland expressing business. I thought that it was something that we should do a couple of times each year but since it was most unpleasant for him and kind of painful, I knocked off the twice a year thing and thought that it might be better if I waited until Butch told me that he had a problem while scooting across the floor.

Jeff Marginean

CHAPTER 7

Policing the Perimeter

I enjoy hanging around the house and doing odds and ends in the home improvement arena. Call me crazy but I guess you could say I'm a "home enthusiast." I saw this phrase written in an ad for one of the large home improvement chains and thought it was stupid but if the shoe fits … that's it! Anyway, my favorite projects are always outdoors and if I know I have inside repairs or projects to do, I will usually put them off until the weather starts turning bad in the winter months. Having Butch with me while working outside was a clear bonus. He was by now my permanent shadow and he would always hang around, chewing on something and watching what I was doing while I was working. I liked having him out there with me even if I was on the tractor mowing the lawn. Having a riding mower, I had to put him in the house when I was mowing because the last thing I wanted was to be watching him run into the street and get hit by a car while I could not get off the mower fast enough to stop him. Also, I did not want to have to stop working every two minutes when he was out of sight to find out what he was up to. I didn't like the idea of tying him up to a rope because when he ran after a "visitor" in the yard he would get yanked by the neck like the dog in the cartoons! How could Butch maintain and build his tough-guy image being tethered to a pole like a commoner. No self-respecting ruler of any domain would allow this, so I'm quite sure he would make short work of chewing through anything I tied him up with, except a chain. No ... being an engineer, I had to be more technically inclined to keep him within our boundary and have him feel as though he could run free. This called for a modern solution. The famous Invisible Fence® was the answer.

Now, I know that there are many people out there, animal activists and pet societies alike, that do not like the use of shock collars for any reason at all and that warn against the use of these devices. Also, I had no intention of strapping any type of shock-anything to Butch without first fully investigating the pros and cons of the device and looking for other possible alternatives. While I was researching different types of containment, an incident occurred with Butch that convinced me of the urgency to find something fast.

Dad had brought Buttons over one Sunday afternoon and we were standing in the driveway watching Butch and Buttons play in the side yard. As we were standing there, one of the many neighbors with a dog walked by with their small white dog. When Butch saw the dog, which was slightly bigger than he was, he forgot everything he was doing and ran right into the street to greet the people and the other dog. Luckily, there wasn't a car in sight. Nevertheless, I thought, *We can't have this.* Living on a corner lot with plenty of passersby walking dogs will surely lead to a catastrophic incident sooner or later. He really needs to know his line in the sand and I would have to draw it while he is young. I have never hit Butch, but I came real close to spanking him for not listening when I called. I did holler at him though and that seemed to be enough to strike fear in his little heart. I proceeded to place a little black and white shivering ball of fur into his cage in the house. I know he didn't know any better but I felt like I had to mark the occasion with an unpleasant moment for him. Oddly enough, I recalled the phrase "It hurts me more than it hurts you," of course referring to that famous line that most parents give a kid who's about to go to the woodshed for an "educational adjustment." It's true. I did feel bad. Another life lesson learned. Looking back, it was a good day for us both, a turning point in our life together that would yield a satisfactory lifelong solution for us both.

The very next day I called the Invisible Fence distributor and made an appointment. One good sign was that they were really booked up and they could not come out for a couple of weeks. By this time, I had already started walking Butch around the yard three times each day on a leash along the perimeter of the yard where I wanted the fence line to be. Wanting to maximize the area that Butch could run and travel, and my lot being nearly a perfect square, I could make the line about ten feet from the street on both sides of the corner and make it about two or three feet inside my property line on the sides of the backyard, giving him almost the entire lot size as his "kingdom." By the time the Invisible Fence representative stopped by, Butch was doing pretty well, staying inside the yard and not running into the street. I had started to teach him to come when I whistled so I could give him a treat. He was pretty good at coming every time I whistled for him but I knew I still couldn't trust him to be left alone outside. He did seem to know that I had placed a limit on him and he seemed to be OK with it, but one dog walking by or a rabbit, squirrel, or cat across the street could have easily lured him into a chase. I sat with the rep at the picnic table on the back patio and we talked for a while about what I wanted to do. The fellow was clearly a dog lover and was very patient while I asked him many questions. He noticed my concern of not wanting to hurt Butch and wondering if he was too small yet to put this giant medieval device on his collar so that I could administer electroshock therapy or hit him with this stun gun like a criminal. He laughed and said "We put these collars on dogs that are three or four pounds full grown. Butch is more than twice that size now. He will be just fine." I thought, *This guy must think I'm really a idiot to have these concerns.* He took some extra time to give me examples of other dog owner's concerns and assured me that I had nothing to worry about. He was confident that Butch would do just fine with it. It lessened my concern somewhat to know that smaller dogs had this collar and that this fellow had extensive experience with them.

At that time, because it was October, they had a few different special deals to choose from, trying to get the fences sold before the winter ground freeze occurred. Since a couple of training sessions went with the package, I went ahead and made the deal right then and there and gave him my deposit. He, in turn, gave me a training video, some materials to study, and reassured me that I would be very happy with the results. He also made the statement, "Butch is already pretty smart and Boston terriers in general are very intelligent. You will be surprised to see how few times he gets shocked before he 'gets it' and knows his line." I thought to myself, *We'll see.* I had serious doubts that this would work and feared that Butch would be constantly getting shocked. I scheduled the installation for a couple of weeks in advance, making sure I could get the time off of work to be there when they came to install the underground cable. I wanted to make sure the line went exactly where I wanted it to go. In addition, being an engineer, and an "outdoor home enthusiast," I wanted to see the machine that they brought out to bury this cable.

A couple of weeks rolled by during which time I watched the video, read the material, and did more research on the internet about the success rate and possible problems with the fence. This was so that I could ask more questions and try to cause Butch as little pain as possible. The installation tech was right on time and I walked him around the perimeter while he painted little white lines on the grass to follow while burying the cable. He then went back to his van, and unloaded quite a large apparatus with a lawn mower engine and a spool of wire hanging in between the handles. It probably took him all of five minutes to install the buried cable in the exact position he marked. He made the indoor hook up, handed me a collar, I gave him the check for the balance, and after he placed little white flags around the entire perimeter marking the buried cable he was gone. The whole installation took about forty-five minutes total and if it hadn't started to rain while he was installing the buried cable, no one would even have known he was there except for the flags he left behind. So far, I was very happy with the service, the professionalism, and the manner in which the whole deal was handled but I still had my doubts as to the validity of the concept. The next step was the training that was scheduled for a week later, after I had the opportunity to work with Butch, teaching him to stay away from the flags while he was wearing the new collar.

I began working with Butch as soon as I could after the line was installed. The only thing that deterred me was that the weather was starting to get cold and rainy and I was worried that I would train him now and then have to train him again in the spring. The collar that the installation fellow had given me had rubber covers over the metal prongs that protruded from the receiver on his collar. He told me to make sure I could get a finger between the prong and his neck, that way it would not be too tight around his neck. I thought OK, so I used my thumb! The method that this collar employs is a warning beeper followed by a very short jolt after three beeps. The initial part of the training consisted of me leading Butch into the "beep zone." Then I pulled him back and ran into the center of the yard or the "safe zone," away from the flags, rewarding him with the obligatory "Nice boy, good boy" spiel. I was to do this in all areas of the yard so he would know the flags were all the way around the house and that they marked his line.

On a cold October morning, the guy that does the training stopped by for the first training lesson. I thought it would be a good idea for Dad to see this because if it worked for me it would work for him also. Being eighty-one at the time, Dad could not be running through the neighborhood trying to chase Buttons down if she decided to take a stroll on her own. On this first day of real training the gloves were off and the rubber covers came off of the posts on the collar. It was *go time*. We brought Butch out on his leash with a fifteen foot rope tied to it and let him wander around. It was going well but the fact was after about ten minutes of walking Butch never went near the flags or the line! The trainer said, "He must know what the flags mean already." He started moving toward his truck and Butch started to follow him and walked right into the line on the driveway and received a jolt. He yelped and I pulled him back out of the field. This was his first "shocking experience." I don't think he really knew what to make of it. He kind of sat there looking at me as if to say, "What was that all about?" I began walking him around the yard while the trainer was shaking the flags saying "No" at each one. Then he instructed me to throw a ball or something and play with him in the "safe zone" so that Butch would know that it was OK to be outside instead of bolting for the garage. After seeing how fast he ran across the yard, the trainer made a few adjustments to the collar telling me that he was turning down the amount of time it takes after the beep for the shock to activate, only giving him one or two beeps instead of three or four. He said that Butch and other types of these small terrier dogs are so fast that they can potentially run through the entire field before the collar will even activate, so he had to "take it up a notch." To this day, as fast as I have seen Butch run after squirrels and rabbits, I have no doubt that he could still run right through that field and not even get a beep. The only thing that stops him is that he knows where his line is and he thinks that anywhere outside his area, unless I am with him, will give him a good jolt!

Now that I have had some prolonged experience with the whole setup and have seen Butch react to different situations, in the last couple of years, I can honestly say that the Invisible Fence is the best investment that I have made for his safety. The sales rep was correct. I bet that Butch has not been shocked more than five times in the last three years. He will not approach that line even without his collar. He is always aware of where he is in relation to the line and knows the boundary all the way around the house. He will not chase a ball, a flying disc, an animal, and most importantly, he will not come to anyone that may call him if they are outside that line, even if they have a dog with them. I never let him outside without the collar unless I am with him throwing a ball or Frisbee for him to catch. All other times, he does have the collar on and he can go in and out of the house at will. Even though he knows the line, I believe, from watching him with and without wearing the collar, he does know what it is for. I have seen him walking the perimeter around the house testing the line. He walks with his head down sniffing the grass and all of a sudden the collar will beep and he just takes one step back in and never loses a step. When he was little, not yet a year old, he would let out a yelp and run to the garage even when he heard the beep while I was holding the collar in my hand. Seeing him "policing the perimeter," and learning that he was actually that smart and had caught on to the line so quickly, was very interesting. I began to see that Butch was going to be keeping me on my toes when it came to outsmarting him.

Maintaining the integrity of that line is foremost in the long-term success of its containment. This means following the directions for taking him for a walk every time *all of the time*! When going for a walk, I was instructed to pick him up, take him to the other side of the street, and then put him down in the same spot every time we begin a walk. It is this spot we must return to when we come back from the walk and I pick him up to bring him back into the yard. This has to be done at the exact same spot coming in or going out. Now, Butch is pretty easy to pick up but a bigger animal is definitely a different routine. Regardless, this still must be done at the same place. You cannot cheat and walk the shortest distance across the yard because you have to maintain the illusion that this is the only place we can cross over the line. All this, naturally, is to be done without the collar on him while crossing the line. One other important item is to remember to take the collar off of him before putting him in a vehicle and pulling out of the driveway! Otherwise, you will end up with a dog that is not only afraid to go outside the yard but also afraid to go anywhere in a car also!

It wasn't long after Dad saw how the fence worked, and a heart-sinking incident with Buttons wandering off in his neighborhood, that he decided to get one also. Buttons is a sweet little dog who is playful and inquisitive yet relatively delicate. Dad, as octogenarians go, is still quite spry and active. Taking the time to spoil Buttons, and give her the great care that she gets every day, is what keeps him going every day. The thought of losing her was just as unbearable for him as losing Butch would be to me. I'm quite sure he would never forgive himself if something happened to her.

One summer day I received a frantic phone call at the office from Dad saying, "Buttons is gone, maybe the neighbors took her! I saw them with a towel wrapped up and they got into their car ....And now she's gone." He had called me just after getting in the car and going around the block looking for her. I spoke to him for a few minutes and drove over to his house. When I got there, there was Buttons standing at the door looking at me and preparing to jump all over me. Dad had said that the lady at the end of the street had brought her just after he had talked to me on the phone. He saw the woman gardening when he drove around the block and told her just to call Buttons if she saw her and she would come. You see, the houses on Dad's block are back to back and running down the length of the city block are fences, garages, and shrubs behind each house. Buttons, while sniffing around in the backyard, started following a scent or something behind the neighbor's garage and probably lost her way before she knew where she was. Dad said she was really trembling when the lady brought her back but that was all the convincing that he needed to get the electric fence.

Even though these Boston terriers are very intelligent animals and Buttons had never gone out of the yard before, I think that the Invisible Fence has prevented many other potentially tragic incidents from happening to Buttons and Butch. Since the arrival of Bosco, Butch's little brother, from the same mother and father, Buttons and Pudge's second litter of pups, the Invisible Fence was the only thing standing between a happy house and a disaster. Bosco, who has very distinct bulldog traits, has trouble written all over his face and ever since he could walk he has been a pistol. Dad's Invisible Fence has kept Bosco alive. I really have to recommend this to everyone who wants a more carefree and better trained dog.

Jeff Marginean

CHAPTER 8

Grooming, Dating, and the Chick Magnet

Trying to figure out what Butch and I could do together away from home outside of a walk has always been a challenge. Aside from going to the pet store, where he would be welcome, I could not think of any place else to take him. There are a few dog clubs around where I live in Ohio, but you usually have to drive some distance to get to them and even then, with some of them, we could only do outside activities a few months out of the year. All things considered, the pet store was the best place to go and hang out. When Butch was only two or three months old, I would take him to the store a couple times per month. He was much too small to let him play with the other dogs and he was actually afraid to be there. The floor was pretty slick, and the fluorescent lights were so bright it was like being in an interrogation room. I can imagine that a place that big was scary for him at first, so I would try to take him there for grooming and getting his nails trimmed to help him get used to it. Leaving him there only seemed to upset him more. He would shake and shiver so much that I felt bad. It didn't seem to make much sense taking him there to be groomed if all I was going to do was walk around the store for thirty seconds and then hover in front of the window so he could at least see me. Without even realizing it I had become the "hovering parent" worried about the little guy because he was so scared.

Feeling like I made the decision to "home school" my kid, I learned to give him a bath, clean his ears, and trim his nails by myself. I noticed right away that he was more relaxed and even seemed to enjoy taking a bath. I think that it was because he likes to play in the water so much. I had a few thoughts about his fear of going elsewhere to be groomed which included these: maybe they were a little rough with him, maybe they clipped his nails too short and it hurt, or maybe he got soap in his eye once and he never forgot it. Whatever the case, it definitely was not Butch's favorite place to be. I think the problem was more with Butch than it was with the groomer. I thought they always did a nice job with him and he always came out looking and smelling great. I suppose that I had to learn how to take 100% care of him myself for a few good reasons. The most important of which was to be able to give him a really good, close, periodic inspection while bathing him and make sure he is doing OK and had not picked up any undesirables. I'm sure the groomer would mention any problems but I thought that it was important for me to know how to perform these tasks for Butch so that when we went to training he wouldn't be the stinky kid in class. In addition, when I did the math, I would be way better off buying the materials to do this myself rather than paying a groomer to do it every couple of months. With what I paid for one visit, I could buy a good expensive dog shampoo, which would last at least a year, and a good expensive nail trimmer! Yeah, doing it myself was a much better idea.

Although I dreaded the prospect of wrestling with him and chasing a wet dog through the house, once I started grooming him myself, I began to see that it wasn't as bad of a task that I thought it would be and I even began to like it. I know he enjoys it now because I take a little extra time for him to get used to the blow-drier sound, which he never really liked at the groomer either.

Unfortunately, this was one less reason that I needed to go to the pet store and mingle. To make matters worse, I started noticing what a fuss the girls would make over him when I did take him to the store. The fact that these types of stores were not around when I was growing up points to a whole new frontier in meeting women. I never really made the connection of the mathematical formula (cute little puppies) = (female attention). How stupid of me not to pick up on this faster. Whenever I would walk around carrying Butch through the aisles of the store, inevitably someone, usually an attractive female, would walk right up to me and give me that swoon, "Awww, what a cute little puppy, can I pet him? What's your name little guy?

How old are you? I want to take you home with me!" Butch, without fail, would play right into it, peeling his ears back and making his already bulbous eyes even bigger and licking the hand of his new admirer. Come to think of it, I could probably learn something from him. I've never tried licking the hand of someone I just met. I mean, I've tried everything else, maybe that would work … or I would probably be arrested! I don't think I could get away with it like Butch does.

Even though he is no longer a tiny pup he still charms the ladies. My only problem is that I don't know how to take it to the next step without feeling like an idiot. I never used to have a problem talking to females and I am generally a personable guy and not too overbearing. I think I might need psychological help at the university research level, possibly a whole team to study my regression as I have aged. Butch just looks at me and shakes his head as if to say, "What's the matter with you? I'm doing all the work here and you can't even get a lousy coffee date! Tsk! Tsk!"

It all kind of reminds me of the time I met my sister Jeanne for dinner after I had just picked up my new stylish glasses. Hoping to charm the good-looking waitress, I began a conversation with her in a semi-flirtatious tone, introducing my sister so that I could clear the path for an introduction of my own on her next trip to our table. As I was showing my sister my new specs, the waitress returned with our dinners and noticing them in my hand the waitress asked "Oh, those look great. Are they new?" *OK, she is showing some interest,* I thought, *this is good.* My reply was "Yes, as a matter of fact they are." "Let me see you with them on," she requested. Not being able to keep my mouth shut and just put the stupid glasses on, I wanted to demonstrate the durability of the frames that the sales person gave me in her sales pitch. "They are the new type that you can bend and they will not break!" I explained as I twisted the frames around. Just then, much to my dismay, and to the amusement of onlookers, the lenses popped out of the frame up in the air and landed squarely in my steaming hot pile of steak and chicken fajitas. A moment of silence … then an ear-piercing eruption of laughter from my sister, the onlookers, and the waitress. I had to laugh also, as the only thing I could think of to say was "Well, at least I can see my dinner better!" Again the laughter escalated from those around us who had witnessed this "spectacle." Needless to say, I didn't ask for the date nor did I go back into that restaurant again any time soon. Maybe I should have, maybe she thought it was cute, but with my manly pride and freshly bruised ego, I just couldn't see myself starting a relationship on that note, so I quelled the possibility.

It's these types of first encounters that everyone can recall in their lives from time to time. For me, I guess they just became more frequent as I started to lose my touch in talking with the fairer sex. So, for a long time, I typically avoided those situations as much as possible. I think a lack of confidence is easily able to creep in once you allow the gift of gab to be stifled. Minding my own business was the order of the day and I followed it to a tee. I followed this credo maybe too well sometimes, being accused of being a snob. I had turned into one of those people who became more closed in and shut off from the outside world. Butch, however, was trying his best to change all this, running up to greet anyone and everyone he could in all situations and venues. Actually forcing me to speak to people and answer their questions.

I soon began to buy one little cheesy plastic toy after another just because we went to the store to walk around on a Friday night. You might think that this is strange but before you pass judgment, I think you would be surprised at the number of people who do the same thing! I would be interested to know how many couples have actually met in a pet store with their pets actually making the introduction. It's almost the best place to meet new people. You immediately have something in common.

Before I knew it I had a huge mound of toys that Butch didn't play with and usually after a few trips, you begin to see the same people time after time. When I was beginning to tire of the whole experience, I noticed that the store offered all types of training classes for dogs. They had classes for puppies, beginners, intermediate, advanced, and other types like agility and "click-a-trick." I thought this might be a good idea for Butch, just to get him away from the house during the winter months when it is really too cold for him to be outside at any length. I suppose it was also a good reason for me to meet new people and to let Butch mingle with other dogs. It sure couldn't hurt getting *me* out of the house a little more often. On my next trip to the store, I stopped to talk to one of the trainers, Cheryl.

She was the same person who helped Dad figure out what food to start feeding Buttons when we first brought her home. She introduced me to Leslie, who is the other trainer. We talked a bit about the available training courses and I introduced them to Butch. He was about five months old at this point so he immediately made a great impression! About one week later, I enrolled Butch in his first puppy training class even though he was a month or two older than was required in the class. I figured that they wouldn't mind since he was just a little guy anyway and they didn't. I thought that the class would be easy but little did I know that the adventure was about to begin. As far as meeting new people was concerned, especially females, Butch continued to draw them in and roll his eyes just before I walked away. What a team!

Ahhh … the human romance. Nothing else in life is like it and nothing compares to it when it is good ... or bad. There are as many different attitudes, beliefs, and opinions about dating in every form as there are people in the world. In our increasingly isolated society there are, in my opinion, fewer and fewer places to meet someone. Don't get me wrong, I do believe that it can happen anywhere and at any time and for many people it has but you would have to admit that with the rise in crime and hearing something on the news about people turning up missing on a monthly basis, internet dating, the bar scene, and night clubs can be risky. Meeting in a social situation where everyone is with their dogs immediately lightens the tension, gives an opening to conversation, and leads to introductions to many different types of people. It's great fun for the animals also! Having Butch around to do these things with definitely makes life a little more exciting and I can see where people who lose a spouse or are otherwise alone in life can benefit from having a pet of some kind to interact with on a daily basis. Meeting others with pets is just as much fun for Butch as it is for me.

With Butch as part of my self-contained little family, I feel that I now have to consider his feelings in the matter of which person I do and do not associate with. Oh, I know some people would think that this is crazy, that Butch is a piece of property not a person whose feelings should be considered, but I bet there are just as many people who would be on my side on this subject. It's not like he is wearing a purple robe sitting in a velvet chair with a great big oracle cap on his head while I bow down seeking his approval for the next woman I would like to date. The robe is orange and the hat really is not that big. I don't even think he has a purple robe! Just kidding! But I do think that his feelings should be considered because I have no intention of giving him up for any reason or any person … period! I'm not prejudging anyone, nor am I ruling anything out but a I have to start somewhere! It's hard to imagine that Butch wouldn't like just about anyone that I would introduce him to. He is a very loving little tough guy when you get to know him. I'll just have to be careful to add Butch to my selection process of women that I date. Just as I'm pretty sure that most women that I would date would probably do the same thing with their pet.

I have read books where people say that you have to treat

dogs just like people. I have read other books that bash people for treating their dogs just like people because they are animals! I think that in many instances it is probably better for individuals to treat their dogs like a person because there would be less chance of abuse and a little more respect for its life. However, I do see the merit in the opposing argument, that dogs are animals and they do have instincts, but regardless of this they are still a long way off from what their ferocious ancestors were. Yes, they are animals, but dogs of all domesticated breeds have been so selectively bred, not to mention inbred, for so many generations that our dogs could not last in the wild for more than a couple of days even if they used those natural instincts that have been watered down after hundreds, if not thousands of generations. There are naturally exceptions to this rule as some dogs just naturally are not far off from their ancient ancestors. Sled dogs come to mind and there are others, but even the hardiest of these could not last in the real wild for long. They would end up something's dinner, or freeze to death, starve to death, or die of thirst. Yes, they are animals but in most cases they are what we as humans have turned them into. It is now up to us to care for them because without us they will die. I don't think treating a dog like a person is a bad thing at all, at least not from the standpoint of providing the basics of life and maybe a little fun in between.

There will inevitably be people that go overboard with this philosophy, lavishing their dogs with extravagant gifts, clothes, and unnecessary accessories that simply ease the tension of the owner and do nothing for the dog. There are those people who replace their otherwise absent mate with a dog in order to fill an emotional gap. They spend enormous amounts of time, energy, and money for the betterment of the dog's quality of life. Although outwardly this may look like a good thing, in some cases, I'm afraid that it is not healthy for either the person or the dog, leaving no room for another person to enter the picture at a future time.

I do know that there are women I have dated in the past who are absolutely not "dog people" and if I had married one of them, I probably would not have been able to have a dog at all. I'm not sure if it was that they were allergic to dogs, were bitten by a dog as a kid, or just didn't like dogs. I never thought to ask because I didn't have a dog at the time and the subject never came up. Looking back, I can say that I'm glad that things turned out the way that they did. I know now that I *am* a dog person and will be for the rest of my life. Especially since Butch has gone to all the trouble to teach me so many things.

Pets and dating are almost like having kids and dating. Many of the same questions come to light, such as will Butch like this woman? Will this woman like Butch? Will Butch try to claim her by peeing on her new shoes? Will Butch latch on to her ankle if she has a cat and he smells it? Does she even like dogs and if so does she have one? If she does, will Butch get along with her dog? On and on it goes. There are a multitude of questions with seemingly a million different answers, much of which can be filtered out by asking another question: Is this someone that I might consider marrying? Because let's face it, at my age, looking to get married and have kids is the only reason to be dating. I have absolutely no trouble keeping my days and nights filled with projects of all kinds. Some of which include Butch. So, that having been said, it is safe to say that anyone that I date would have to have some sort of amicable relationship with Butch lest there be a major problem between us. Not caring much for arguing, I am more the type to just forget the whole thing rather than get into an argument that neither side will win. Not wanting to have an anti-social dog, it was necessary for me to dust off my shelved social skills. Regardless of all the details, Butch has reintroduced me to the world, dragging me behind him one giant step at a time!

Jeff Marginean

CHAPTER 9

The Smartest Dog of All Time

Butch is smarter than your dog and all the dogs that you know and any dog that has ever lived since the beginning of time and there will never be another dog smarter than him … until he is gone and I get another one! I hear some form of this statement from virtually everyone I talk to who has a dog. On rare occasions, some people will say, "My dog is as dumb as a box of rocks!" Generally it is these types of statements, smart *or* dumb, that I hear and in most cases it is usually true. It's an obvious sign that people love their dogs when I hear them say things like this and I will usually go out of my way to humor them because I know that Butch is really the smartest dog in the world! Just kidding! Whether we think our dogs are smart or dumb shows at least that we are paying attention to them. It does not mean we love them any more or less, given their level of intelligence, and when we get a new puppy it is hard to tell how smart or dumb they might be or if they will need to wear glasses. Our dogs really don't care how smart or dumb we humans think they are. They just want to love us. It is, however, interesting to watch puppies develop and learn new things. Whether they are smart or not they are bound to learn something. Noticing what Butch has picked up as he has grown has been remarkable to me. Probably because this is new territory for me and I do find it fascinating.

Butch, as dogs go, is no idiot. Butch, as some humans go, is a genius. In fact, I have read, and have been told, that Boston terriers are one of the smartest breeds around. Not having much experience with other dogs and minimal experience that I can recollect with Babe, my first Boston terrier, I felt that it was something that I was going to have to see for myself. I know that I have gushed about how amazed I am when Butch does something that shows me that he is a "thinker," but truthfully I believe that my amazement stems more from the fact that I have not had the experience with dogs the way many others have. There are many dogs that I have seen, including service dogs that help the blind, that are absolutely amazing in what they do and how they do it.

Just think of it. There are dogs that are called "service dogs." These dogs can actually think and anticipate the needs of their owners sometimes before the owner even knows what he or she wants. These dogs can be trained to help people in a multitude of ways that I find incredible. There are guide dogs for the blind, hearing dogs for the deaf, support dogs for the handicapped, search and rescue dogs, and even crime-fighting dogs, and I'm not talking about "Underdog" either! There are therapy dogs and dogs that help autistic children … I mean, it is incredible what dogs can do. Not to mention guard dogs and the dogs that work on farms and herd animals! Trainers and breeders of these dogs know which ones will be best suited for each type of work. They try to pick the best of the best of the litter, those that will conform to the training and programs needed to develop these most helpful of "man's and woman's best friend." Many people I have met already know much more about the seemingly endless things that dogs can do for people but being that this is all new to me it's like having Bigfoot walk up behind me and slap me on the back of the head!

These dogs notwithstanding, Butch ranks right up there as pretty darn smart in my book. I know that I am a little partial and that Butch can't do many of the things that other dogs can do, but I don't think he *wants* to do the things that other dogs can do anyway so he is still pretty smart. Trying new things with him all of the time and having him catch on quickly, proves to me that he is very intelligent. He doesn't go for that chasing the flashlight or laser pointer on the ground stuff, while I jump up and down telling him to "get it!" He will just look at the light or red spot on the floor, look at the source in my hand, and then look up at me like he is saying, "Do I really look so stupid to you that you think I would chase that?" He will usually just turn around and walk away as if he's thinking, *Whew, who's the moron here?* So much for the cutesy fooling the dog for a laugh antics. He is much too smart for that. I will have to put much more thought into the effort than swirling a light on the carpet.

Learning the proper way to train Butch is as much a part of the process as actually working with him. Butch is just like a sponge waiting to soak up anything I can teach him. Everything is a learning experience for him. Trying to stay one step ahead of him, introducing new toys, new games, and thinking of things to keep him occupied, is a fun assignment for us both. After running out of ideas, I thought it was time to seek out a professional.

After signing up for the eight-week beginners dog-training class and trying to get ready for what was needed, the day finally came when we were off to class. It was actually an evening class and Leslie was the trainer who would be teaching me to train Butch. As I sat there listening to the initial instructions, I started to get that feeling in my stomach that you used to get as a kid on your first day of school. I know this experience was supposed to be fun but at that time I thought that there was no way that I was going to be able to teach Butch anything, much less learn how to do it correctly. I thought to myself, *Leslie is really wasting her time with us, Butch.* But since the class had been paid for already I knew Leslie had to do the best she could with each of us in the group. Earlier, I had already been able to teach Butch how to sit, stay, and fetch. At five months, he was a little older than the other dogs in the class but he was still a pup and could get a little anxious at times. I knew that there was something that I was missing about how I was teaching him but I didn't know what. Although feeling a little self-conscious about being in the class, I was as attentive as I could be, after work, at 7:00 p.m. on a Tuesday night in December. Butch on the other hand was a massive ball of energy wanting to meet every single dog and person in and around the training area. It took him awhile to get used to seeing the people around the ring before he settled down and paid attention to me.

Once he had greeted everyone and said hello to all of the customers in the store, he would start to pay attention to the class. After about forty-five minutes of the class he would start to run out of steam. It's really a lot of work for him to greet everyone and all the other dogs! Whatever the reason, he would just shut down, as if to say "Well, that's it. I've had it and I'm too tired to do anything more so I am just going to lay here until we leave." This would happen just about the time when we would start to perform leash training. You know, training your dog to get used to the leash and to walk nicely by your side without pulling. Luckily after the first class I had invested in a few training aids that Leslie mentioned would be helpful. One of these items was a training harness that went around the dog's front legs and chest and not around his neck. Being a Boston terrier, and a puppy on top of it, Butch's little square noggin and scrunched-in snout were way too small to use one of the gentle leader type collars that fit around the mouth and head.

The harness style collar I bought for him was not cheap but it was worth every penny. When Butch tries to pull while wearing this collar and I am holding the leash, the harness pulls his front legs off the ground but it doesn't hurt his neck and throat. Dogs that have the pushed-in face are already susceptible to breathing problems so I thought it would be better for me not to be the cause of any external injuries from a collar. The whole idea of a good collar was to teach the dog not to pull while walking. The package that the harness came in never said anything about having to drag your pet around the training ring on the smooth polished floor because he refuses to move!

So, there we were, everyone laughing, kicked out of the training line because Butch decided he "had enough training for that night" and just laid down "frog-legged" on the floor. In the following couple of weeks, he decided that he was not going to walk at all for any reason. Leslie would even change the routine and make us walk first but Butch had decided that he was not going to walk until *he* was ready. Did I mention that Boston terriers can be as stubborn as bulldogs? Many mistake this stubbornness for stupidity in these breeds but let me tell you that they are not as dumb as they want you to think they are! We were sequestered to the outside of the ring and I literally had to drag Butch around each lap on the smooth floor like a dust mop while he was frog-legged flat on his stomach. Sometimes I think he did it just for the attention. He would pop his head up as he went sliding past customers and onlookers as I dragged him across the floor. Much to their delight and amazement, they all would burst out laughing while Butch just hung his tongue out and went along for the ride. He would walk at home just fine and he understood my commands when we would practice but he just would not listen when we got to that training ring. As plainly as I could see Butch's defiance, I could see the lesson in patience that I was being taught also. It was a battle of wills and I kept reminding myself that there was no hurry for him to learn, that he would lose this battle, and I would keep telling him that he *would* lose! This only seemed to strengthen his resolve. That little snot just did not want to cooperate. It was a total of three weeks before I finally "broke him!" God bless Leslie and the patience she exhibited during that training exercise. I could tell she was a real professional by the way she understood dogs and gave each of us her complete attention when were having a particularly hard time. She really went out of her way to help us individually as she navigated through each portion of the course. Even she got a big laugh out of Butch not wanting to walk! It was a hilarious sight.

Once he realized that he could not win the walking battle, he began to walk on command and did just fine. Little did I know about the next scheme he was cooking up. Bolting off to meet the other dogs on a whim! One night about halfway into the training, we were doing the sit-stay-come routine. Butch would sit, and would stay, but when I said come, he would run right out of the training ring to greet the nearest dog he could find or try and grab a bag of treats off of the shelf. After a couple of tries, Leslie blocked the doorway and had a few people stand around him. She told me to make a real big deal when he comes to me and give him a few treats while petting him, saying "good boy!" OK, so here we go, I told him to sit. He sat. I told him to stay. He stayed. I walked about fifteen steps away, turned to look at him and said "come!" He just sat there and looked around, plotting his escape no doubt. Watching him look around I knew his little wheels were turning again. When playing, he would not make a move until he thought about it for a few seconds. When he realized that there was no way out, he decided to come to me. I thought, *Finally! He is starting to listen!* As I bent down to greet Butch with my rather robust frame, I heard a very low, rather lengthy tearing sound and immediately felt a refreshing breeze against my undercarriage. *I just ripped my pants.* I looked up and tried to play it cool as there was nobody standing directly behind me, so I didn't think that anyone noticed. I'm sure the expression on my face changed but it could have been attributed to my thinking Butch did not do what he was told. Leslie came over to me to reassure me that he did what he was supposed to do and I whispered to her, "I just ripped my pants. When I walk away, let me know if you can tell." I walked back to my spot in line with Butch and looked at her and she shook her head no. Then I was not quite sure what she meant. Either no, she could not tell that I ripped them or, no, I can't believe you actually ripped your pants! I ended up walking backward for the rest of the class and, no, I did not have to buy bigger pants. The pants ripped because they slid too far down off my waist before I bent down. No, really, it's true! Being winter, it made for a rather drafty ride home! From then on, it was sweatpants and sweatshirts all the way.

Taking Butch to training every week and working with him every day in between took some getting used to after a tiring day at work. But that little face, and those big eyes, so excited to see me every day when I came home, gave me the extra boost of energy I needed. How could I refuse him? Oh, brother! Now I was really starting to turn into one of those "nummy num" people again.

After a rough start for the first few weeks, Butch began to catch on pretty well. We did so much together that it was almost as if he was anticipating what I wanted him to do. He was learning at an incredibly fast rate and I have to be honest when I say that I was wondering how long it would be before I could teach him to speak. Yes, literally speak; you know, recite the Gettysburg Address and things like that! Seriously, I think that being one-on-one with him definitely helped speed his learning process. Since I was the only one giving him orders, feeding him, and playing with him every day, he was pretty focused on me and I could teach him just about anything I could think of. He was only too eager to do whatever I expected of him and this was the factor that helped his learning. Most dogs are very eager to please their masters in any way that they can. They are always looking for that pat on the head, the treat, and even the "good boy!" that goes with it. The main trick is for them to recognize who is their *one and only* master. More than one master or an unclear chain of command in a house full of people is very confusing for a dog.

Wanting to please me is especially true with Butch since I'm all that he really has. He lives for me. He always wants to play, is always loving, and is always in a hurry to forgive me if I have to holler at him, hurting his feelings in the process.

This is his nature. It remains true to this day that our bond has become stronger because of the training classes that we took and continue to take together. It was especially important for me to control my own antics as well as controlling Butch. No playing tricks on him like fake-throwing the ball then hiding it or pinching him when he was sleeping. If I pulled any shenanigans while he was so young, then the trust that we have built would be gone. It would make him not only harder to train but stressed out when he is around me. Such treatment could even make him afraid of me. I think that I was learning as much as Butch with every week that passed and controlling my pranks was difficult if not sometimes nearly impossible but I can say that I have so far been successful in curtailing the tricks. I always had to make sure that every time I said "Go" to him that there was always a ball, a Frisbee, or something flying to meet him at the other end of the yard. As his trust in me began to develop I sometimes dropped the ball by accident and he would stop and look at me or come trotting back to me, somehow knowing that I did not do it on purpose. We would set up, and he would take off again when I said "go" as if nothing ever happened. Also, I noticed over time that he would not flinch when I came into the room, like he did when he was really young, straining to see who it was or what was going on. At this point, even when he is sleeping, Butch does not flinch when I get really close to pet him or even go nose to nose with him. He just opens his eyes, looks at me as if to say, "What do you want? Can't you see I'm trying to sleep?" This type of trust could have never developed so fast if it were not for the structure of the training classes and

96

Leslie's patience in teaching me small tips and tricks which I used to help Butch develop. The class lasted eight weeks and we had a good time going through it. Leslie was very nice to everyone and gave me many new ideas on how to properly train Butch. I did meet many new people and their pets, which also started conversations on how to handle certain situations with our "new additions." This was an unexpected perk of getting involved with a training class. The amount of information that you can learn by just talking to other new owners is enormous. It kind of gives you a support network while you are trying to figure things out with your new companion. Socializing Butch with other dogs and people as much as possible during this time was also a side benefit. Getting him used to others at a young age was more important than I realized at the time. His friendly attitude toward others is a direct result of these classes.

After having such a good time with the first class and now that Butch actually learned how to walk without me having to drag him, I thought we could sign up for another class. Being the dead of winter, it seemed like a good idea to get him and me out of the house as much as possible. I felt that the agility training course would be a good choice for him since we both like to roughhouse when we are at home and he is definitely full of energy in the evenings after sleeping all day. Being that we had a few weeks until the class was to start, we went back to our routine of visits to the pet store, just to mill around and talk to people. There are always a few interesting people with their dogs to talk to. Agility training consisted of taking the obstacles, one at a time, introducing a new one each week. The second half of the class was dedicated to adding the new obstacle to the previous week's obstacle and running the course. Naturally, the object of the class was to get the dogs to learn to take each obstacle and go through them one at a time in succession. In this particular class, Butch was one of two small dogs and was very excited to run up to the larger dogs and spring to his hind legs, grabbing the other dogs by the head with his front paws and licking their faces. He didn't seem to pay much attention to any of the smaller dogs in or around the training area. Butch, as I have come to find out, thinks that he is seventy pounds and thirty inches at the shoulder. I don't have the heart to tell him how small in stature he really is and I have removed all of the floor level mirrors in the house!

CHAPTER 10

Size Matters

Butch has an affinity for big dogs. I'm sure part of it is that he thinks he is much bigger than he actually is. He thinks he's a real tough guy when we are out in the yard and another dog, no matter the size, comes strolling by, walking its owner. It doesn't matter to Butch how big they are. He just wants to give them what-for in barking dog language for even thinking about walking past our house. What he really wants to do is declare our corner property its own country and charge people tolls for walking by. He surely is cantankerous for as young as he is and he doesn't hesitate to show contempt for the smaller dogs either, snorting and growling as he stares them down. Maybe it's that he doesn't have any respect for dogs that he knows he can handle if he needs to. He is very sneaky also, luring people with their pets into our driveway or lawn. He will crouch down like he is cowering with his ears pulled back and those big soulful eyes opened as wide as they will go and just when they get inside his line, close enough for him to reach, he explodes into a jumping-running maniac. He knows he can't go outside the fence line so he has learned that, if people see him, he can put on this act to lure them into his grip.

Take for instance the little furry Chihuahua, Dooly, that lives next door. He stands just out of reach of Butch's line and barks at him in Spanish. If Butch is playing with his big ball, he just ignores him which makes Dooly mad and a little adventurous. He will run into the yard as fast as his little legs will carry him, run right up to Butch and bark right in his face and then run away, back to his driveway. Butch ignores him most of the time but I did see Dooly run up to Butch and nip him while Butch was playing with his ball. I ran over to grab Butch but before I could, he took off after Dooly and walloped him a good one tackling him before he made it past the line. I grabbed Butch quickly because I was afraid he would hurt him or worse. Since Butch feels it is necessary to kill anything he can catch running through the yard, I was afraid he might take this attitude with Dooly or any other dog that might stroll through the yard, especially those that taunt him. Since Dooly is so small, I feared that Butch would mistake him for a squirrel, especially when it's dark outside. I've seen Butch chase dogs that were three or four times larger than he is out of our yard and they actually run away from him! Dad has told me that while Buttons and Bosco run into the house, he has seen Butch chase a wandering German shepherd out of his yard on more than one occasion. Perhaps the reason Butch is not afraid of larger dogs and prefers them over small ones is that I am so much bigger than him. He is rarely around small dogs, so he probably looks at me like I'm a big dog!

Going to training classes, meeting other people, and playing with the other dogs, I noticed a marked preference in Butch for extremely large dogs. Rottweiler, Great Dane, English bulldog, boxer, or any dog at least twice his size is usually his target as soon as we get into the store. The smaller dogs, meaning any weighing less than thirty pounds, Butch usually ignores or will generally tolerate if there are no "big buddies" around to play with. He even ignores the little "yappers" unless they get right in his face, in which case he always tells them off and tries his best to get at them as we walk by. It is really funny to watch a little three-pound Chihuahua march around barking like a little drill sergeant and see Butch ignore him, that is, until he's had enough and Butch takes out after him to shut him up. I usually have to watch pretty close when Butch is around dogs his size or smaller. Butch is over twenty pounds and stands at about thirteen inches at the shoulder, but he is built like a little tank and he is tough as nails. He has a very tender disposition with people and most other dogs unless they take a posture with him. It's almost as if he says, "Oh, you want to mix it up do you? OK, I'm game."

Butch is really not the type to look for a fight but, being a type of bulldog, he will not back down either. He has a real stubborn streak and a thick head so if he latches on to another dog, or anything for that matter, he will not let go. He is one of those dogs that you can lift off the ground while he is gripping something in his teeth, just like in the cartoons. I'll bet if you listened close enough you could even hear him snicker a little. OK, so I watched a lot of cartoons as a kid! Being that he can easily support his own weight with his jaw, and has fun doing it, you can imagine how difficult it might be to pry his teeth open when he has a death grip on something he doesn't want to let go of. Like another dog for example. I try to discourage this and Butch usually does listen pretty well but I still worry about his attitude when other dogs or animals wander into the yard. It has been my experience that it is difficult to try and train this behavior out of him. I think that it is just part of his personality. A dog is a dog and should be expected to act like one in all situations.

Like all people, Butch has his ideas about where he stands in life and that is something I can thank myself for in many cases. Being that I trained him, I have shaped some of his attitude also. This, however, can be a good thing in the long run. For example, when Butch hears something out in the yard or outside the door, he will erupt in a snarling, snorting, barking frenzy you would hear from a much bigger dog. There are many people who are now afraid to even walk in the driveway because "Butch knows we're out here!" Let's just say that he sounds like the vicious dog on the other side of the fence and when all you can do is *hear* him, you will think twice about climbing that fence to get to the other side. It's comical to see the size of Butch after hearing him "voice his opinion" from inside the house. I have had people approach me and Butch when we are outside and ask me where my other dog is. I look at them puzzled and say, "What other dog?" They would reply, "We walked by your house last evening after dark and we heard a much bigger dog barking from inside." I would just smile and point to Butch. I would tell them that he does have a pretty big mouth. "When Butch opens his mouth his whole head disappears!" They would say, "No way – that little guy couldn't make all that noise!" Some did not believe me but all I had to say is come by the house again and knock on the door and you will see for yourself. No one has yet to take me up on it but sooner or later they will realize that it is just Butch and that he can get pretty scary sounding if he wants to.

In my current circumstance Butch is exactly the right size for my lifestyle. He is small enough that he is very easy to take care of and big enough to play rough, catch a Frisbee, or chase a ball. He is small enough to jump up on me and curl up in a chair and big enough that I can pet him if he lies next to my recliner on the floor. He is small enough to move around the house very quietly yet big enough to jump on my bed in the middle of the night and shake the whole thing. He mainly does this during the winter months when he gets chilly at night. Having the thermostat programmed to go down to sixty-five degrees all night long, Butch will burrow under the covers and snuggle up next to me. He is small enough to push his head up under the covers without waking me up and big enough that I can't roll over on top of him and squish him while sleeping. What is really funny is that I have a giant, king-sized bed on which I pile all of the pillows that I don't use on the opposite side. Most mornings I will wake up and hear Butch's distant snoring thinking he is in the next room sleeping on the chair. When I get all the way out of bed I cannot quite tell where the snoring is coming from until I look down at the pile of pillows and see one little rear dog leg sticking up through the pillow fort that Butch had fashioned during the night. Other nights, he will just burrow under the covers and as I roll over he follows which leaves me sleeping on the smallest edge of the bed and him continually trying to push me off. In addition, sometimes he will burrow under the covers and turn around laying his head on my pillow so that we are nose to nose. Then he wakes me up when he starts snoring. It's not that he is claiming the bed for himself. He is just being a dog and when dogs get cold at night they huddle together for warmth. He wants to stay close to me for heat. He never wakes me up on purpose except on the rare occasion when he needs to go outside, in which case he walks on top of me, jumps off the bed, and rings the bell hanging on the doorknob. The bell is his signal that he needs to go outside. He has a heart as big as an elephant in a gallon-of-milk sized body. He is the perfect sized little buddy.

Knowing that Butch is partial to larger dogs and possibly wanting to expand our little family in the future by adding another member would be quite an exercise for us both. Even thinking of getting another companion for Butch might be somewhat of a touchy situation. Butch is pretty much in charge of his area here and to introduce an interloper might be a power struggle, unless it is done correctly.

First, figuring out the type of companion Butch would enjoy the most is not really difficult. It would have to be a dog that, once it was old enough, could play with Butch and keep up with him. Therefore, a puppy would be the best way to go. I am not against adoption and I am a big advocate of the adoption agencies but at this point in our lives adoption would have to be carefully planned to ensure the type of companion best suited to Butch and my lifestyle. Having any new puppy at all would definitely change things even more than Butch himself initially did. The only problem with any new addition is that someone would have to be with them almost all the time while the puppy was small. I'm not too concerned with Butch hurting the puppy because he has always seemed to know how to play carefully around little ones. I would be most concerned about the puppy learning bad habits and having them reoccur in Butch. I would also have to strictly maintain the rank and file. If not kept in check, keeping me at the top of the pecking order would be difficult and would need to be enforced. Without doing this, there would surely be problems and more fighting than necessary between them. Having them both understand that I am the alpha dog will lift some of the pressure on them both and eliminate most of the competitive fighting for the top spot.

Contemplating another addition to our family brings up a

dilemma in that handling two dogs with my current schedule is unreasonable for me and unfair to both dogs. I would not be able to give them the quality of life that I can now give Butch. It is unfair to impose two dogs on Dad a couple times each week instead of just Butch and it is unfair to them to leave them alone too much all day long. After the pains that Butch and I went through to get him comfortable with my routine, I don't think that I could handle another dog at this point in time. Not only that but I might eventually like to breed Butch one day and have one of his sons after he is gone, just to keep the blood-line going. Fighting the urge to get another companion for Butch is only a matter of using some common sense. Does he even want or need a companion with Bosco and Buttons around? I get the feeling that he does like to go see them but he also likes it when it is just the two of us. I do know that he likes to sleep all day when I am not home also! If I get a companion for Butch now and also want to breed him I will eventually end up with three dogs! Did I say three dogs? I get tired just talking about it! I would have to move to the country to do that. That is not a far-fetched idea. There is plenty of land I could buy in northeast Ohio but it is way too premature to be thinking about that right now. If I got another breed, what would it be? Maybe I am way too analytical about it but I have thought about it some and I believe that I have narrowed my choices down to a couple of breeds that might fit the bill.

Butch's new buddy could be an English bulldog or a boxer. Seems like both ends of the spectrum doesn't it? In many ways they are except that Butch has one thing in common with them and that is that they all have some bulldog in them. I have something in common with them, as far as that goes, which is probably why I like these types of dogs so much. I have a cousin, Sherry, in California who breeds and raises champion boxers so I am sure that if I were to decide on a boxer she would definitely steer me in the right direction. I think a boxer would be great. The only drawback that I could see would be that a boxer, I think, would be just like a giant Boston terrier. With all of the energy Butch has I'm not sure I could handle a "giant Butch." As a boxer grew into a large sixty-pound dog towering over Butch it might lead to a few confrontations. An English bulldog, although also quite a load at sixty to eighty pounds, might be a better choice because even full grown it would still stand about eye to eye with Butch, albeit three times as wide. From Butch's standpoint, I think he could handle a bulldog better because he would be much faster and a bulldog might be easier to play and wrestle with. On the other hand, a boxer would be a good choice also because he could keep up with Butch catching a Frisbee and would be generally more athletic. There are also the predisposed health problems that each breed is susceptible to that I would have to take into account when making an educated choice. It is not a light decision to make for such a long commitment.

In either case, the most important thing is that we would all get along well as long as I do not slack off on the training. Their failures would always be my responsibility and getting them the basic training that they should have will make them and me happier in the long run. When it comes right down to it, either breed would be a good choice and once again it would depend on the amount of quality time we could all spend together. I'm sure that any new pup would fit right in and would learn many new things from Butch. It would be exciting to watch them continue to grow together and it would keep me on my toes training both Butch and his new buddy. Although it is not the right time yet, the day will come. And until then, my buddy Butch and I will keep doing our thing together. Bulldog or boxer, we'll see which way the wind blows when we're ready.

CHAPTER 11

Dead Already?

Ever since I first brought Butch home, I have had thoughts of the time when he will be gone. I am not the type of morbid person that needs to be miserable to be happy, quite the contrary, but this topic could not be avoided once I knew that I was responsible for this little life that had been placed in my care by a seemingly automatic series of events. I suppose a little worry about this issue is a natural reaction for many new dog owners ... I mean dog parents! After all, if you are any kind of decent human being, you are going to put some of your heart and soul into the care and nurturing of this new member of the family. Even if it is only a family of two! There are literally millions of unwed dog owners out there, like myself, who may have come into dog parenthood before they even knew what hit them. Maybe the passing of a friend or loved one left a dog homeless and you couldn't bring yourself to just take it to a shelter or dog pound. Maybe a dog was left in the care of someone in a will or possibly came from friends or family who just could not take care of it any longer. Whatever the situation, if you care at all for this dog you will become attached quickly and will potentially worry about the day that the pet is no longer with you. Sadly, there are many new owners who only have their dog with them for a very short time, through no fault of their own. Accidents do happen and unforeseen natural sickness, sometimes, does end in the untimely death of this special new friend. A certain amount of concern is warranted but if it becomes a constant, unending, paralyzing worry then I would say it is time to seek some professional help on the matter. If you worry too much about it then you could end up with a trip to the macadamia ranch!

I guess it's more of a reflection on life than anything else. For me, it was a wake-up call for my own life in the sense that I never really thought about it much, especially so soon after Mom's passing. When someone close to you passes away, there is a certain numbness that follows you for a period of time. I think most people who have experienced this would agree that for a certain amount of time during the mourning process everything is just numb and void. Having Butch introduced into my life at this particular time helped me progress out of a sad season and put me back on the road to steady recovery and a new, albeit strange, life. Looking at Butch, watching him grow, and the fact that this is a one-on-one relationship, I suppose I was drawn closer to him knowing that he relies on me to be there to take care of him every day and night for the rest of his life. This fact draws me into a line of thinking about not only what would happen to Butch if I was gone, but what it will be like for me when he is gone. Not having a "pet" experience like this before, I'm not sure if this is a normal reaction or not. I guess that, being the same as most human beings, a certain amount of sad feelings about a day that we all know will come, but do not like to talk about, is a normal part of life.

It leads me back to the day when Dad had to put Babe to sleep and how hard it was for him to say goodbye. I know I felt bad back then and I'm sure I missed Babe but being only ten or eleven at the time, I don't remember how I handled it. I don't recall crying about it then but I don't think that I can say that I wouldn't get emotional when Butch's time comes. I think in many ways getting older does that to you no matter how "hardened by life" you think you may have become. There is always going to be something that will crash through that wall and let out the emotions. Many non dog owners probably do not understand the attachment that can form between a pet and owner and may think that pet owners are nuts or weird for getting so attached to an animal that they treat it like a member of the family. It's fruitless to try and explain it to them and not worth getting worked up about it. They have their own ideas and it's still a free country. At least it was the last time I checked.

For the millions of single people out there that either have a dog or obtain one, this addition to their "family of one" fills a void of loneliness that simply cannot be explained. Older people who have lost a spouse, people who are abandoned by their mate, single people who have never been married, people in special circumstances who get specially trained dogs as helpers, I mean the list can go on and on. All of these people develop a special bond with their dog and each one is as unique as the individuals involved. In my case, I was pretty content with my life before Butch came along. I worked. I did my personal projects, which took up most of my time away from work. I helped out Dad with miscellaneous things and that was it. Being single made it easy to move around and go places. Butch opened up a whole new world for me with respect to socializing, training, and caring for him that I never would have experienced otherwise and it was a welcome and pleasant change. Being content with where I was in life, I saw no reason for change. Seeing no reason for change, I would just move forward doing the same things day after day, living for myself and not really "giving anything back to life." Butch has made me a contributor, more so than I could have been without him. Wanting to do things with him and for him, watching him grow and learn new tricks, and just hanging out watching TV together creates a bond one stitch at a time that most onlookers will never understand!

For a single person, it is different. Talking to Butch as if he knows exactly what I am saying is a normal everyday occurrence. With the look he gives me sometimes I expect him to start talking right back. I know he thinks about things, because he usually pauses before he acts in most cases so I know the little wheels are turning in his head. I recall hearing somewhere, and I don't remember where, that dogs can learn and retain the meaning of over 200 words. I would never have believed it before having Butch around. It is amazing what dogs can learn all by themselves. They are just like us in many ways. They have feelings that can be hurt, they are happy and sometimes sad. They think about things, maybe not like we do, and it may be for the short term but they do, nevertheless, think about things. They certainly know when they have done wrong and most of this is based on your reaction to them. Which, in and of itself, is unbelievable in the way that they pick up on our intricate behavior. Some of it, I'm sure, is instinct, but mostly I believe it comes from simply being with that individual day in and day out. This relationship is no different from being in a house full of people who are family members, learning their intricate idiosyncrasies one day at a time. The only difference is that dogs generally have to put up with the things that irritate them because they can't leave the house without you! There really is no reason why dogs cannot be considered family members or treated like a part of a family unit because frankly they are and they should be.

It's this everyday-life contact that makes the bond between a dog and its owner similar to having another person around – so similar that it is almost impossible not to share a bond at some level. It's this reasoning that makes me wonder about the absolute idiots I see on TV who have a dog tied up outside and actually let the collar grow into its neck, requiring surgery to remove it. In medieval times they used to make the penalty fit the crime. In cases like this, that doesn't sound like a bad idea.

I am not some "crazed" activist but I do enjoy animals and nature and think that they should be preserved as much as possible. For the most part, we are very lucky to live in the world we do today. In the case of owning pets, they should be treated in most circumstances with the respect they deserve. If raised correctly, all that most dogs want to accomplish is to please their owners. They want to be with them as much as possible and will be by your side all of the time, just hanging out with you. They don't even care what you are doing as long as they can be near you. The long and short of it is that they are the ones that nurture the bond that develops and they need this bond as much as we do, maybe without even realizing it.

Butch has literally grown into my life and is an integral part of what I do every day. He lives for me and waits for me every day to come home and play. He is always looking for the next opportunity to be around me. Whether it might be to sit when he is told or to retrieve a certain object that I ask for, he is always at the ready. He is quick to forgive and happy all the time. He is my best friend. For someone who does not have kids, I guess that this is a similar situation to what kids and fathers might have for the all-too-brief period of time that they are kids. I know I enjoyed seeing my Dad come home from work every day when I was little, that is, before I was old enough to be in any trouble! The point is that whether he can talk or not, Butch speaks volumes in our relationship and the day will come when his big-little heart will stop beating, the house will be silent, and that physical bond will be here no more. No other dog can take his place. Just as no other person can take the place of a beloved family member who has passed on. He is *Butch*, and there will never be another. Will we see each other again someday? Do dogs have a soul or spirit? From my point of view, I would have to say that they do. I know that I would like to think so, but that is another subject for another time.

Jeff Marginean

CHAPTER 12

Dog Sitters

When Butch was a mere couple of months old and I took him home for the first time, I had the opportunity to introduce my "new addition" to the neighbors. Living on a city block, most of the houses have connected backyards which are very well defined mainly because of the age of the area. Trees, shrubs, and decorative fences abound in the well manicured area where I am fortunate enough to live. There are many retired people living in my neighborhood whom, if the truth be told, were the ones who actually built up this area, making it one of the nicest little cities in Ohio. There is nothing particularly special about it except that it is a very clean, well-kept city with a great school system. It is a terrific place to live and raise a family. There have been many young families beginning to move into the area over the last fifteen years or so and I have had the pleasure of meeting some of them.

It is a great neighborhood and one of those great families lives catty-corner to my backyard. Ken and Cheryl with their daughters Danielle and Christine live in the house with their black lab mix Lilly. They are a hard-working all-American family. I have often said that if I ever have daughters, I hope they turn out as well as Danielle and Christine. I have watched them grow since they were just little kids playing in their backyard. We attend the same church, although at different times, so I do run into them there occasionally but mostly I see them outside doing yard work or walking or jogging with Lilly carrying her leash in her mouth trotting along side.

Introducing Butch to Lilly for the first time was entertaining to say the least. Butch, being just a tiny little thing, was easily intimidated and probably terrified of Lilly as she would trot behind him trying to get a sniff while Butch ran for his life to hide behind the trash cans. The seasons were changing from fall to winter at this time so the outside encounters were very limited for a number of months until the weather finally broke in the spring. Over the winter period, Butch was grew rapidly and was starting to claim his domain, announcing it to any animate or inanimate object that would pass by including but not limited to cars, people, blowing leaves, and even trash cans that would magically appear on the curb the night before garbage collection day. He was becoming the ruler of his space and he began to adjust his newly developed cocky swagger for outdoor use, trotting around the house like he owned everything.

It wasn't long before the weather started getting warmer and the end of school approached. I would usually start doing some outside work, cleaning up fallen branches in the yard from the winter storms and starting to estimate what it would take to get the outside of the house back into shape for another warm season. Butch was always by my side, trying to take the sticks from my hand and grabbing the bottom of my pant leg as I dragged him growling across the lawn. Carrying his ball or Frisbee, he would taunt me with it, daring me to try and get it from him. He had gained much confidence in himself over the winter and being almost one year old he had grown tremendously during the secluded snowy months that we spent inside and going to training.

Seeing how much Butch liked to be outside and play, I started to feel bad about having him cooped up inside the house all day long during the upcoming nice weather. Aside from the twice-per-week visit to Dad's house for a romp with Buttons and Bosco, I felt that it just wasn't fair that he couldn't be outside as much as safely possible. Trying to think of an acceptable alternative to keeping him in the house, I thought it might be nice if Danielle and Christine were not already working during the summer that I would ask if they could "dog sit" for Butch. This would allow him to run around outside in the nice weather and it would be a great help to me, in that I would not have to go home for lunch and let him out every day.

I asked and they accepted. Like any parent, I did set a few ground rules. Butch always had to have his collar on when he was outside, no matter what. The reason for this was that even though he knows the girls, he can still be very stubborn and may decide he doesn't want to listen to them. During the excitement of play, he could possibly take another exit route across the street in front of a car while trying to get away from them. The collar rule was for the avoidance of a potentially sad situation for all of us. The other rule was that they couldn't walk him around the block. The girls and their parents were avid walkers and joggers and were used to walking or jogging through the neighborhood almost daily. There is nothing wrong with this and it's not that I didn't trust them with Butch. It's just that since he was only about a year old, I did not want him getting too familiar with the neighborhood or being away from the yard without me. It may be kind of paranoid but the fact is that if he was taught that the yard and house were the safest place in the world, then he would be uncomfortable anywhere else without me and would naturally avoid going out of the yard at any time even without the collar. Largely due to Butch's smaller size, and the length of my yard, it is not necessary for him to be walked around the block for his daily exercise. He does enjoy a good walk around with me but he would much prefer to chase down the Frisbee 100 times each day for his workout.

This was the setting for the summer. The girls would come over, bring Lilly with them, and they would all play Frisbee or throw the ball in the yard, giving them all a good workout. It was during the course of the summer that I would learn the extent of Butch's growth over the previous year.

It seemed that he would no longer take to cowering behind the trash cans at the mere sight of Lilly. Instead, realizing that he was becoming as fast or faster than anything in the yard, he began to turn into a slobbering Tasmanian devil. He had begun to use his natural endless energy to literally freak everyone out! Jumping up on everyone and buzzing around everything so fast that all they could see was a black and white blur! I'm sure that Lilly was even taken aback by Butch's quick movements as she approached him in the yard. She was probably wondering where he came from and if he was the same little dog she saw the previous fall. Being older than Butch, Lilly would kind of just stand there and wonder what the heck he was doing. Butch was simply showing off, as if to say "Look at me, I'm over here, now, I'm over here, pretty fast aren't I – don't you want to chase me now, c'mon chase me, chase me!"

CHAPTER 13

The Tri-Athlete

Boston terriers are not supposed to be the athletic type. Even the AKC places them in the "non-sporting" group. I'm sure they have their reasons and I'm admittedly no expert but I'm still not sure why. They are as fast as anything out there that is their size. They are definitely just as strong if not stronger than any twenty-five pound dog could be. They have the same instincts as other small hunting terriers, so why the brush off? Maybe I should qualify my statements by replacing the word "they" with "Butch." Much of his athleticism comes from the way I raised him. Wrestling on the floor, teaching him to catch a ball, and teaching him to catch the Frisbee probably account for why he is like he is. I thought that playing with him this way would keep training fun for him and also help to burn off some of his enormous energy. He seems to gravitate toward the rough side though which can be a little troubling sometimes especially when he is around small kids. He does seem to know his limits with the children and frail older people once he gets past his excitement. As he gets older, he seems to know in advance when he needs to be calm around those who are not as athletic as he is. He is even very gentle around small puppies, which was evident when Buttons had her second litter of pups. Butch would sniff them and wait until they would start to jump on him. He would then roll onto his back and let the little puppies jump and crawl all over him playing. He knew that he could not be rough with them and was surprisingly gentle. With a puppy's heart still beating inside him, my buddy Butch was growing into a strong young man … um … dog. Blazing speed, lightning reflexes, and an endless will to run all rolled up in a black and white artillery shell package. Non-sporting group? Somehow I just don't think so. Even from the time Butch was very tiny he would chase anything that I threw, bringing it back to me as fast as his little legs would carry him, sometimes smashing right into me sitting on the floor.

I started throwing a Frisbee for him to chase from the time that it was nearly the same size as he was. He instantly knew what to do with it, bring it back, lie at my feet and try to chew it up while keeping me from getting it. As he quickly grew, it became more of a taunt for him to come into arm's reach and then whip around as I reached for it. After hundreds upon hundreds of throws, he started jumping up to knock the Frisbee out of the air. Being too impatient to wait for it to land, he would start jumping up to meet it in the air. Now, he didn't start catching it but I never thought that he ever would. I honestly thought that he would just keep the object of the game *get the Frisbee once it had landed* and bring it back to taunt me with it. It took me by surprise that he would actually start catching it on the fly sometimes in an acrobatic jump. Most of the time, I would make a bad throw or he just would wait for it to drop, but it has now reached the point where he is so excited to play that on the first few throws he will jump and catch the Frisbee in his mouth, stop on a dime and return with it. The funniest part of this Frisbee game was that sometimes the disc would flip upside down and he would pick it up and run back with it. The only problem was that it would flip up over his face and he could not see where he was going. This didn't even slow him down but it did lengthen his trek back to me by adding a zigzag step to see what was in front of him by peeking around the disc. As I would talk him back to me, it looked like he was drunk, staggering back to me with his yellow disc flipped up over his head. Anything to get that disc back to me as there is always a treat or some fun waiting for him when he arrives at my feet.

The tennis ball is the old standby for just about every boy and dog in America. Not being a boy any longer but not wanting to deprive Butch of this heritage, I picked up a few tennis balls of varying sizes to see what he could do with them. I noticed two different types of tennis balls. The tiny ones and the larger regular sized ones. Butch made quick work of the small ones, after one throw and a couple of chomps those little tennis balls were in about six pieces as I hurried to get them before he swallowed any of them. Well, that was not going to work. Even the larger tennis balls I purchased at the pet store were not up to the task either. Those balls are not true tennis balls and are not filled with enough air to make them difficult to puncture or even bounce very well for that matter. In my effort to get the ball from Butch's jaws, he would chomp down on that ball so hard that it always blew the seam out, which in turn ended up in pieces also. Real tennis balls were the answer but although Butch liked to chase them they were a little too fuzzy and he didn't seem to like the taste so he would not go get them after a few throws. I really didn't think he was going to be a tennis ball dog until one day I was walking through the pet aisle at the grocery store and found mint flavored tennis balls. I thought that was kind of peculiar but realized that someone at some pet product company recognized the same problem that I had. These balls were hard like a regular tennis ball and you could smell the mint right through the package. These were definitely worth a try. After trudging through the rest of the grocery store retrieving the staples of the week, I drove like the wind … not like I had the wind … but drove like the wind to get home.

Butch always knows that when I get home from the grocery store, I have something for him. He also knows that I go to the grocery store on the exact same day every week. This routine has prompted him to prepare for something good. So after putting things away and changing clothes, we were ready for a game of ball. I was in the process of teaching him the difference between the front of the house and the back of the house. Standing in the driveway at the end of the house I would point to the front yard and say "front," and then throw the ball over the roof into the front yard. Butch would go scrambling into the front yard sometimes beating the ball, catching it on the first bounce, or skidding to turn around when it hit behind him. He grabbed the ball and started to run back and then stopped. Spit the ball out and sniffed it. I thought, "Well, that's it. He doesn't like it." He picked it up again and ran right toward me … and right past me into the garage so he could gnaw on that new mint ball. It turned out that he really did like it.

This gave him and me one more thing to do and I was able to teach him the difference between the front of the house and the back by just using the words "front" and "back." Now when I let him out, all I have to say is "front" if I want him to go to the front yard. The only problem with this is that there is a move that they teach dogs in the intermediate training classes called "front." This is to make the dog walk behind its master and sit, facing front on the master's right side. So now I can't use that word since he knows that means the "front" of the house. Being that Butch is a medium to large size Boston, he has a mouth in that little square head of his that is plenty big enough to not only carry that tennis ball around but I thought he could also learn to catch it. This was another activity that would keep him thinking. I tried numerous ways to teach him to catch, all ending in an excited jump, hitting the ball in the air with his snout. Thinking about this for awhile, I decided to try the step approach, starting with regular small liver treats. Putting the treat about two inches from his nose, I would say "Ready?" then I would drop it into his mouth. I would do this over and over until I could tell he was opening at the right time. I would make the distance greater until I could throw them up in the air anywhere near him and he could catch them. I was always mindful to say "Ready" before each toss so that I would have his full attention. This took a few days for him to get good enough to catch them from about five feet away. Once he could do this, it was time to go back and teach him to catch the ball.

Knowing that it could possibly hurt him if I threw it at him and it hit him in the face, I started the same way I did with the treats, about two inches from his nose. When he could catch it from about twelve inches away, I moved away from him and started bouncing it once on the driveway until he started to catch it. This only took one day after teaching him to catch the treats. Now it never ends. He always wants to play catch or have me throw treats in the air for him to catch. There is no end to his trickery also. There are many days when I come home really exhausted from work and just want to sit in the chair and vegetate. Well, Butch will have no part of that, running to get his football so we can play as soon as I walk in the door. As he hands me each of his toys and I drop them to the floor one by one he still doesn't get the message. He thinks, "Oh, he doesn't want to play with this one I'll just bring another one until he likes it!" About the time that he has transported every toy from his room into the den, he starts to understand that I don't want to play. He begins to snort in disgust and circles the room in front of my chair. He then meanders over to the door, stands up on his hind legs, and rings the bell to go outside. Knowing that I will get up from the chair to let him out, he usually has a plan to do one of two things. He either jumps into my chair as I am putting my shoes on to go outside with him or he will grab a toy and jump up putting it in my hand. He can be a little shyster if he wants to be. In either case, I have to laugh. It is very amusing to see him demonstrate how his mind works.

As fall weather yielded to freezing cold winter days again, the outdoor activities were limited to Butch's daily relief and the occasional romp through the snow. This is hardly the weather to be throwing Frisbees and tennis balls around the yard. Even though Butch was always at the ready and staring at the "outside toys" on the shelf in the garage, being the responsible "parent" that I was I couldn't see keeping his shivering little body outside any longer than necessary no matter how much he whined. I will say that there is the occasional incident where I run through the house, Butch nipping at my socks, and I open the door to let him out. As I run past the shelf in the garage I will grab his disc and run outside throwing it across the yard into about six to twelve inches of snow. He will take off after it as fast as he can, bring it back to me, and stop to relieve himself. We then go running back into the house. On a good snowy weekend this will happen three to six times each day! I make it quick so he doesn't get too cold, yet we can play outside for a few minutes at a time. It's a game because he never knows when I will jump up and run outside! No matter where he is in the house, if he hears me rumbling through the living room, he knows it's *go time* and is right on my heals! Indoor sports were next on the list and the porcupine football tournament was very appropriate. You see, I have never had too much trouble inventing my own fun and now that Butch was with me I thought it was time to dust off my game invention machine and go to work to keep him busy.

After going through the training courses and recalling some of the things we did in the agility course, I stopped at the toy store one day and bought Butch a tunnel. It was green, had a little flap at the end but it was long enough that I could make it curve. I made some simple little jumps for him as he would exit the tunnel. I naturally had to think of a method that would give him maximum exercise with minimal effort on my part. After all, I wasn't going to run around the course with him. The tennis ball turned out to be the perfect answer.

Butch was never particularly fond of the orange tunnel that was used during the agility training class. I'm not sure if it was the surroundings or the color or even the texture of the material but he had a hard time getting through it. He didn't much like the new one either but I knew that I had enough patience to train him to run through it no matter how long it took. Every night after work, we went down to the basement after dinner to run the course. At first it was slow going. He was very timid and unsure about walking into the tunnel. I did not rush him and eventually he would go through it on his own, but he would never come back that way. After I knew that he could go through it I introduced the tennis ball into the game. Throwing the ball through the tunnel would force him to run through the tunnel to chase it but he would always come back on either side of it. Being the superior intellect that I am, I decided to block off his return path so he could not get back to me except by coming through the tunnel. Butch, being the stubborn little "thinker" that he is, had an answer for this that blew me away. I proceeded to block his return path, so that the only way back to me was through the tunnel again, or so I thought.

I threw the ball through the tunnel fast. Butch took off after it, jumping over the two obstacles I had made. He grabbed the ball in his mouth and turned around to come back. He made it over the two jumps again but stopped when he saw that his path was blocked on one side, then on the other side of the tunnel. Wanting to go around the tunnel and not being able to, he backed up and looked at me, then the tunnel, and walked from side to side for a few seconds. Then he stopped and looked at me again, his ears popped up like "idea lightbulbs" on top of his head. He turned around jumped over the two jumps and as I called after him, "Butch, come back here!" he made a right turn at the furnace. He never looked back once, going through the other doorway and coming all the way back to me through the adjacent room with no lighting in the other room! Anything to not come back through that tunnel! What amazed me is that he actually thought about it after he had summed up the situation! Unbelievable! Of course closing the doors to the other room followed. It took a couple of additional repetitions for Butch to realize that if he wanted to continue playing he had to come through that tunnel. Then, he started coming back through the tunnel every time, like he had done it his whole life. He was just being stubborn but in the end it was a good lesson that really made both of us think! It is this type of fun that is the most interesting to me as well as a good challenge for Butch. Seeing what new things he is capable of is what always keeps me thinking up new activities for him to do. He has learned so many things so fast that I should enter him in the triathlon or maybe the poly-athlon if there is such a thing!

CHAPTER 14

Big Balls, Balloons, and Throwing Up

In my never ending quest to find new things that Butch might like to do to keep us occupied, I ran across something that I think all dog owners should try at least once. I was in the grocery store one day and as I was walking through the aisles, I noticed one of those large displays that hold children's play balls. These are the brightly colored ones some of which were a tie-dyed, swirling multicolor. There were small ones that measured about ten inches in diameter and they also had really large ones that measured twenty-four to thirty inches in diameter. I figured that since Butch likes to chase all different types of balls, and makes me throw one a million times every night, it might be interesting to see what he does with these. They are light enough that they would not hurt him and slippery enough that they would give him quite a workout outside in the yard.

Well, bringing the groceries in the house, Butch was naturally excited since he knows that I brought him something. I guess it's like when my Dad used to bring me things some days after work when I was just a kid. He used to bring me little trinkets of various types. Sometimes a baseball, sometimes it was little plastic army men. They were the old-fashioned type that might kill you if you ate the paint. Anyway, when I showed Butch the great big ball that I brought him, he didn't know quite what to make of it. After a couple of sniffs and pushing it with his front paw, he stood there and looked at me like, "What am I supposed to do with this?" Thinking about it for a few minutes while putting the groceries away, I called him outside. Then I showed him the smaller ball and he exploded into a barking jumping fit before I could even set the ball down! He was all over that ball. He was pushing it around the yard until he could get on top of it. Within ten minutes, he had popped it, which surprised me. I didn't think he would be able to pop it that quickly but he was able sink his teeth into it pretty easy. Going through the first ball so fast and still full of energy, Butch was looking at me for additional entertainment. Finally realizing what these new strange larger objects were for, it seemed as though Butch had found his reason for living. I brought the big ball outside and Butch was frantic. He went completely crazy! He hit that ball with his face over and over again from one side of the yard to the other. He would do this until he could get on top of it and try to pop it. In the process of trying to stop this ball from rolling and getting on top of it, he was always trying to press his face into it and get a grip with his teeth. It didn't take him long to learn to roll the ball toward himself while standing on his rear legs. He would do this so that he could find the air hole where they filled the ball. I knew then that he would be able to pop this ball also, as soon as he could get a grip with those little choppers. I laughed so hard the first time I saw him do this that my guts hurt for the rest of the night.

One of the funniest things about this particular car-and-pedestrian-stopping display is that Butch is continuously licking the ball. I determined that he does this to try to soften it up so he can bite into it. Not knowing that he can't soften the plastic by licking it, after literally hours of wrestling with this giant ball, he summons what seems to be hundreds of gallons of self-generated slobber, covering him, the ball, and nearly all of the grass within a twenty-foot radius. This was Butch's new favorite thing to do outside. From that sunny Sunday afternoon to this day, when I want to keep him occupied while I mow the grass or work in the yard, I'll take him outside, throw the ball into the yard and he is good for at least a couple of hours. I eventually was able to teach him to hit the ball back to me. This happened purely by accident one day while I was mowing the lawn. We went outside and I told Butch that I had to mow the lawn. We then went through Butch's normal routine of grabbing my pant leg and growling all the way to the shed, tugging and shaking his head. It took a couple of times for me to realize that, although he wanted to play, it was not necessarily with me. He wanted his big ball. Once I threw the ball into the yard, he was happy and would be busy for at least hour, that is, until the ball got good and slobbered up and it squirted out from his death grip. Usually he would be able to get right back on it but it would sometimes go past his line and with or without wearing his magic collar he would not try to retrieve it himself. He knew it was beyond his reach and was smart enough to come and get me from the mower on the other side of the house. It is this type of response that I consistently see from him that never ceases to amaze and endear him to me, even when I think I couldn't love the little guy any more than I already do. He listens to me even when I'm not there!

I would see him walk around house to where I was mowing, slobber dripping from head to toe, and he would stop and stare at me and bark once … twice … until I would get off the mower. When I would ask "Where is your ball?" he would lead me to where the ball went over the line, run down and stop about four feet from where it wnet over. It wasn't until I walked to the ball that I knew he had stopped because it went past his line. I said "Oh, I see! You can't get it there." I wanted to give him a treat for not going over his line but he wouldn't take it, he just wanted the ball. I walked behind the ball and in our usual posture, I said "Ready?" Butch barked once and I kicked the ball to him. As I started to take a step to go back to the mower, Butch hit the ball with his face right back to me over the line and barked. I thought he slipped. I kicked it again and he hit it with his face again, right back to me. Then I started to get a little more aggressive with him and not surprisingly he rose to the challenge. Mashing his face into that ball and hitting it back to me time and time again, contorting his quick little body to angle that ball right back to me. It's strange but we started having these soccer matches quite often until he got tired of it and would then catch that big ball and continue his quest to pop it!

After going through nine or ten of the larger balls, and the stores being out of them for the upcoming winter season, I ended up having to get him the smaller version once again. This time, however, I was able to find one tough enough to withstand his onslaught of tongue lashing, teeth grinding, and slobber. As I write this, I am sitting about twenty feet away from Butch on a unseasonably hot 84 degree October day here in Ohio. It has taken him all of about four minutes to develop his usual foam beard in addition to adding a thick coat of slobber on the ball and the surrounding grass. It will be one of the last days I will be able to give him a good hosing down after his workout. The weather has been unusually warm these last few weeks, which brings to mind the global warming issue. I don't spend too much time thinking about it though, especially when I see that the record heat for these same days was set back in 1952. Since it has not been this hot here in nearly sixty years I don't see what the issue is ... except money, that is! Well, in any case I think Butch doesn't really care and we are both thankful to be outside a little longer this season than we have been over the last couple of years.

One of the only things that will tear Butch away from that ball is nothing more than just a plain everyday run of the mill balloon. As much as he loves to smash that ball back to me time and time again, I think he loves to hit a balloon up in the air over and over again even *more*. I'm not sure what goes through his little mind while he is doing it but I think he is in some kind of trance. I got the balloon idea while watching one of those video shows on TV in the dead of winter last year. I thought that this would be perfect for him to help beat the winter doldrums which we get during the long cold months waiting for spring to arrive again. We play ball and wrestle around but I know he misses chasing the balls in the yard. Balloons would be interesting but I would have to watch very closely what he is doing so he does not eat any part of it when it pops. Also he would have to learn that they will pop with a loud noise that he absolutely does not like. This way he will learn to back off of them when they hit the ground. I suppose I could teach him this. A trip to the grocery store later that morning would be in order, to procure the next attempt at more Butch hijinks. Now, what color to get? Oh please, are you kidding me? It's more like am *I* kidding me? I stood there in the grocery store wondering what color balloons to get for Butch. I understand that dogs are somewhat color blind so I was thinking about what color I could see best if I could only see in gray scale. By this time, I have recognized that I have officially turned into a neurotic dog dad! I had a blank stare on my face, looking at the balloons, when a very pretty woman walked up beside me with her cart and said, "Trying to pick out a color, huh? Is it a girl or boy?" I said, "He's a *he*." She replied "Awe, how old is he?" I answered "Two." She asked, "What is his name?" I said, "Everyone calls him Butch." "That's cute … Butch! Hmmm, well you have to get blue ones then!" she happily replied. I said "I'm not sure how much it will matter, I think he is color blind." She said, "Oh no, really? I'm so sorry." I told her, "It's OK, I think he has been that way from birth so he probably doesn't know that he is missing anything, I'm just glad he can see. I thought he was blind in at least one eye because one is brown and one is blue." She was amazed! "I have heard of that before, I know it's rare but not really uncommon." I said, "I think the blue balloons will be fine," as I picked up the package of balloons and started to walk away I looked at her and said, "It was really nice talking to you; thanks for helping. I have to go because he starts to get cranky if I leave him in his cage too long." With this I could see her jaw drop and her eyes became as wide as saucers. She quickly pushed her cart to catch up with me and she asked, "Are we talking about a child or a dog?" I looked at her and replied, "You know, I'm beginning to wonder myself! It's my dog Butch!" She said, "You never said it was a dog!" I answered, "You never asked!" We both paused for a moment and simultaneously started laughing. I had made a new friend and her name is Linda …

Let's pause this scene for just a moment and review the facts of this situation. A beautiful woman walks up to me in the grocery store. She starts a conversation out of the clear blue sky. The conversation is engaging, funny, and entertaining and ends up with both of us having a great laugh. Butch was not even there to draw her in. One might think that this is the great beginning to a terrific love story, and it is, if it were not for one small problem. She is married, you see. Where some people have not read the whole rule book, we both understand that when you are married, dating other people is usually frowned upon and generally discouraged except by those who have the morals of a jackass, but we will not get into that right now! In general, what I am saying from a personal point of view is that I get along great with females over sixty, and under twenty. It's the ones in between that I seem to have the problem with, that is, unless they are married, and there is no chance of anything but a platonic relationship.

Now back to the balloons!

Blowing up the first balloon after I got back home and watching the look on Butch's face was an experience in itself. He stood there and twisted his head clockwise as he watched this new kind of ball literally appear out of my mouth.

I looked at him and said, "Want to play ball?" This was the first stupid question that I asked him. As soon as I said this, Butch went into a barking, jumping, and twisting frenzy as he usually does. I threw the balloon in the air and he jumped up and hit it with his face. He would follow the balloon from room to room doing what he could to keep it in the air. Now, Butch is only allowed to get on two pieces of furniture, the recliner that I sit on with towels covering it and my bed. That's it, just two. However, when the balloon is in the air all bets are off and the whole house, furniture and all, is in play. As we run through my house, I turn into a kid again. Jumping and dodging and skidding across the floor to help Butch keep the balloon in the air. He is barking and I am yelling and we are both focused on the balloon. Yes, the balloon would pop on occasion but Butch only popped it twice when it reached the floor before he learned, in the quick fashion that I had become accustomed to, that it would break if he tried to bite it. From that day on, balloons were part of our daily gaming repertoire, and this would burn enough of his energy (and mine) to keep the winter fidgets at bay.

Once the seasons began to change and the weather started getting warmer, we moved the balloon contest out into the yard. Butch excels at keeping it going for a long time. If there were a league for keeping a balloon up in the air, Butch would be one of the stars of the league. He would surely make it to the Professional BKUITAL Hall of Fame. BKUITAL, of course, stands for Ball-Keeper-Up-In-The-Air League. He would naturally be a franchise player and command a high salary as a champion ball-keeper-upper! He has developed into quite an acrobat – twisting, doing near-somersaults, and almost-back flips trying to hit that balloon with everything he's got on every try. He brings himself to the point of exhaustion if I let it go on too long. I have learned to stop the fun before he becomes too overheated or if I see his eyes start to look a little glassed over. When the time comes to stop, I say "OK, that's enough!" Butch heads straight for the showers or rather the hose in the backyard. He knows he is in for a good spray down and a drink of cold water from the hose. This way I can monitor how much he drinks. We then take a cool down walk the long way around the house before I get the beach towels and give him a good drying in the sun while sitting on the driveway.

One rather unpleasant side-effect from all of this activity is the inevitable puking that comes forth if I let Butch go on a little too long, get a little too excited, and drink a little too much water. It doesn't matter if it is the big ball, the small ball that he is chasing from one side of the yard to the other, or the balloon he is punching in the air, he gives it his all. Every ounce of his being is in either trying to pop those balls or in trying to keep the balloon in the air. He gives it everything he's got, one hundred and ten percent and like a finely tuned athlete in training he will work until he throws up after drinking too much water. I call it the "puking Butch two Step." Hit the ball, take two steps, puke. Hit the balloon take two steps, puke … It is not that bad but you get the picture. It took me awhile to understand that his throwing up, after this type of exertion, is much the same as us humans throwing up after doing wind sprints or line drills in training for sports, like I did through high school and college. When the coach wanted to thin the herd, so to speak, and get down to the players that he knew would still be around, we would run line drills and sprints until everyone threw up and some would not return to the next practice.

I can imagine that the feeling Butch gets after playing so hard is much the same upset stomach that occurs in humans after rigorous activity. This being the norm, I have learned to pay careful attention to him during this play time and make sure he is not hurting himself. With all of the slobber he puts on the big ball, and all of the flung slobber during his acrobatic balloon hits, he can get dehydrated pretty fast on a warm day.

While hitting the balloon, I have found foamed up slobber on the middle of his back! This, I think, explains his antics pretty well.

All of this equates to my trying to keep Butch occupied on a regular basis and a side benefit of it is that it keeps me from going crazy constantly thinking about my next project, the next bill I have to pay, or the next thing I have to fix around the house. I guess I have an inherent need to make sure that Butch has a good quality of life now that I am responsible for it. Puking aside, his exuberance for life is infectious. He keeps me in the game and is always willing to try something new that I can think up for us to do together. All things considered, "together" is the most important term.

CHAPTER 15

Trick or Treat

Butch loves kids. This is normal for most dogs I think and especially those dogs who are part of a family that is growing. In most cases, although there are exceptions, most dogs know where they stand in the pecking order. They are generally obedient and are surprisingly gentle around new additions to the "pack" or family in the form of human babies. This is due to the surroundings in which they were trained and the repetitious corrections they have received over the years. In Butch's case it has been just me and him for the most part and the occasional weekly training session that has helped to socialize him to people and other animals. Oh yes, we have the regular visits to Dad's house to play with Buttons and Bosco, his mother and younger brother, to help him be more social with other people and animals – but they are family, and Butch is more dominant around them, being that my Dad doesn't stop the rough play as quickly as I would. I'm not blaming him because I have essentially taught Butch that rough play is OK just by the way we play together almost every day. I am the only one that plays with him like this, so he thinks that it is OK to play with everyone the same way and that we humans all play rough like this. He probably thinks that this is perfectly acceptable behavior and because of his smaller size he can get away with it to a point.

Butch is not particularly aggressive toward anyone or anything but since he knows he cannot venture out of the yard without me, he is *very* territorial and he is not afraid to let anyone or anything know about it, should they decide to take a shortcut through our yard or even innocently walk past. One incident happened on Halloween when Butch was a little over a year old. Although still a pup, he was pretty solid and could expend quite a bit of force if he hit you at a full run, easily able to knock down an unsuspecting child in a plastic flowing Halloween costume. It was a beautiful October Sunday afternoon, one of the last really nice warm days of the year here in northeast Ohio. Leaves were on their way to the ground and the way that I am about the keeping the yard clean I might as well have been out there with a net to catch and bag them before they hit the grass. Milling around in the yard after church with Butch by my side I set out to do a little end-of-the-season cleaning up and trimming before winter. Being close to Halloween, this was the Sunday afternoon that all of the witches, hobgoblins, pumpkin heads, and superheroes *du jour* took to the streets to extort candy from the local residents. This takes place somewhere around 3:00 in the afternoon in our community which coincides exactly with the time that Butch and I were outside.

Up on the ladder cleaning the fallen leaves out of the gutter, I could see the beginnings of the witching hour. Kids and parents alike were coming out of their homes and pouring into the street starting their trek past our house in a bevy of different types of store-bought and homemade costumes. While I was on the ladder, Butch became bored with watching me and while wearing his electric collar began to police the perimeter, noticing an increase in chatter and activity surrounding his domain. Ears straight up and eyes wide open, Butch stealthily walked his post from one side of the corner to both sides of the yard right on his boundary line, seemingly daring anyone to cross it. Seeing that this had the potential to be worse than the previous year and being that it was such a nice day, I decided that it would be best if I stood outside at his boundary line and pass out candy there where Butch knows that he cannot go. This line is his DMZ or demilitarized zone!

I went into the house to get a bowl and chair for the candy when I heard a high pitched-shriek come from the front yard. I ran outside and out of the garage into the front lawn. I couldn't believe what I saw. There was a three-foot-tall miniature Batman lying on the ground, arms and legs flailing, while Butch proceeded to drag the kid by the cape across the yard growling and thrashing his head from side to side.

The kid was struggling to swat Butch with his empty candy

bag to no avail. I got there just as the mom of this little tyke did. "I'm so sorry," I said to her. "I just went into the house for a second to get the candy for the kids." She said that she didn't even know what happened. She never saw Butch in the yard and she turned to talk to her friend and "Wham!" Butch came out of nowhere and pounced right on the kid, knocking him to the grass and grabbing the easiest thing he could, the cape of his costume. Once we knew that both little fellows were OK, I saw a look in the mom's eyes that was surprisingly not upset. They live right up the street so we know each other to wave on occasion but have never talked at length. "Oh, he's OK, just a little startled, I think. Our dog knocks him down on occasion also. It seems like your dog is much stronger than he looks!" She looked as if she was choking back a laugh. From my angle, it was hilarious knowing that Butch would not hurt the little Batman but just wanted to play. From little Batman's perspective, I imagine that it was pretty scary and I imagine it would have been even more terrifying for him had it been dark outside. Butch is mostly black and they would have never known what or how big the thing was that was attacking this kid potentially causing more harm to Butch and the kid. They have made friends since this incident and the little boy rides his bike past the house and says hi to Butch. He will even come up to pet him but only if I'm there.

I don't recall when this activity changed from trick or treating in the evening after dark, like when I was a kid, but I'm sure that the chicken farmers, toilet paper manufacturers, and cleaning companies experienced quite a drop in business at this time of the year due to the change in time for the ritual to take place. In some communities they still have it at night after dark but I guess the daytime switch proved to be good for everyone involved here.

As the day wore on, unsuspecting kids who walked up onto our yard and toward the front door were met with a black and white flash that came running around the corner of the garage to plow right into them. Butch, thinking that he had some new playmates, thought that he would get the upper hand and tackle these kids first and lick their faces once they were on the ground. Well, these kids, not knowing what just hit them, were terrified. Lying on the ground getting their faces licked as fast as Butch could wag his tongue, they probably thought that he was trying to eat their faces off!

Lifting their crying toddlers by the arm, most parents were understanding and knew that Butch was just a pup and did not mean any harm. There were those "dog loving" parents who would just give you the look of disgust, grab their kid, turn around, and walk away from the ferocious fighting Boston terrier that lives on the corner. This is not to say that I let it go on but others that own these excitable little balls of fire know what I mean when I say no matter what you do, they have boundless energy for greeting new people … and kids.

With the small chair and the bowl of candy at corner of the yard, just outside of Butch's line, I could welcome the kids and pass out candy without Butch's over-exuberant greeting. Naturally, the kids really wanted to pet Butch and see him up close but at least this way, if they walked into the yard, they knew he was coming at them. This seemed to work out best for everyone. I could play fetch with Butch between kids and practice some of his tricks for cars passing by and Butch could still greet the kids and get a quick pat on the head between treats! Another indiscretion averted … what's next?

CHAPTER 16

Sounds in the Night

I haven't met a person yet for more than ten minutes who has not made some type of extraneous noise. Whether it is smacking lips, clearing the throat, sneezing, chewing or any other type of bodily function, most living things make noise just by living normally. This being the case, it should not have surprised me when I started hearing Butch's miscellaneous noises, but it did. His noises began when he was very young. Three months old, I believe, is when I started hearing peculiar sounds emanating from his little body at both ends.

During some of the research I was doing before I brought Butch home, I ran across something in one of the books that kind of stated the obvious but it went right over my head. Most people with flat-faced dogs are quite expert at this and must deal with it every so often. All of the breeds that have a short muzzle are predisposed to snoring among other things. Dogs like the pug, the English bulldog, and of course the Boston terrier have what the veterinarians call an "elongated soft palette." This, I'm told, is the cause of some of their breathing problems and is at the root of the veritable plethora of snorts, honks, and snoring that they do on a daily basis. I don't know much about canine anatomy but I do know one thing. Now that Butch is almost three years old, he snores louder than any human being I have ever heard in my life. I can't even begin to imagine how loud a big seventy-pound bulldog would snore. Maybe the volume is not a function of size, but rather just having all of the parts in the right place for the perfect combination and timbre that projects that piercing sound so perfectly throughout the entire house. I don't know how loud bigger dogs might snore but I'll bet that most of them can't hit the level of decibels that Butch does when he reaches a full snoring boil. Snoring, for him, is more of an art form or a sport rather than a problem. He doesn't seem to mind how loud he is but I do recall a few times, as he was growing and working on perfecting his snoring, that he did wake himself up and wonder what all that noise was about. It is not bad enough that he is plenty loud enough to wake me up in the middle of the night no matter where he decides to sleep, but he ends up on my bed at sometime during the night with his face two inches from mine. Once he starts sawing logs, it's all over. It's just like living with another person. I can nudge him or shake him a little to wake him up and like an idiot say, "Quit snoring," but when he falls back to sleep, he starts right up again. Then he decides to move around or roll over on his back with his mouth wide open. It's like I'm in a fifty-five gallon drum with him snoring so loud it rattles the windows! Call me naïve, but I did not know that such a little dog could produce a noise that loud.

This may be my only saving grace and my only opportunity to get a good night's sleep but Butch also has a tendency to bury his head under pillows or burrow under the covers. Summer or winter, he pushes his head under the pillows on my bed. When it's warm in the house without the air conditioning running, his head is under the pillow and the rest of his body contorts into many different positions. His favorite position is on his back with his legs sticking straight up in the air. He does this either under the blanket in his cage, where he comes and goes as he pleases, or on my bed. In either case, I can still hear the strong but faint rattle of those tiny nostrils revving up for a good nose-blasting snore.

The fact that I sometimes wake up with his face just inches from mine brings up another interesting point. It's not always that end that I am staring at when I wake up! You haven't lived until you open your eyes with the business end of a Boston terrier staring you in the face. If you're lucky that's all it will be doing, but that, sadly, is not always the case, which is probably the reason for my waking up in the first place. It is either the slow wafting aroma that finally reaches my nose or the short tearing sound he makes when he peels one off that wakes me up! At the risk of relying on "potty humor" to describe this bodily function I will describe this as delicately as a single guy can. Butch is a consummate flatulence artist. He is decidedly in the upper range of the hearing scale but nevertheless an audible farter of merit. I imagine guys mostly will appreciate this as women refrain from talking about such things in public or usually refer to their own flatulence as "fluffy." As in "Oh pardon me I just made a fluffy!" In any case Butch proves himself to be as human as anyone in this area! Although Butch does cover a lot of area in and outside the house, I can most definitely hear him peel one off at any given time. Usually when he is sitting next to my chair or just generally relaxing. Sometimes I can even hear him from the next room. As with us humans, it truly does matter what he eats. He is a bit spoiled in that department. I try to feed him only the finest dog foods and the only table scraps I give him are steak or chicken, generally only the foods with a lot of protein. If I am cooking some hamburger for sauce or something, I'll leave about a fist full extra rare for him. Sometimes I'll mix some of my restaurant leftovers up for him like some pieces of Prime Rib, rice, and broccoli on a Saturday night. Then once each week he gets a special treat and I'll cook him up a frozen pot pie. You know… the small ones we used to eat as kids. They cost about as much as a can of Dog food and other than being a little high on the sodium scale they generally have good ingredients like carrots, peas, some potatoes, and of course chicken, turkey, or beef. He loves them all and licks the bowl clean every time I give him one. I go the extra mile for him because he is worth it to me. I know some people might think that it is a little excessive but it doesn't happen every day and it really is only once each week. Make no mistake, I know that I spoil him but he is no stranger to good quality dry dog food every day. Although he is not over-weight it is hard to say how the gastrointestinal workings of this particular canine operate. Butch is generally a gassy little guy but much of the time he acts as if it's the first time he has ever let one go. He squeezes one out and then looks around as if to say "What the heck was that?" Like something was sneaking up behind him. Then he looks at me as if to say, "Did you do that?" It's almost as if he thinks someone is standing behind him, the way he reels around. Butch's gaseous antics will continue for many years to come I'm sure, and the ozone above my house will continue to deplete from the methane but his ability to fill a room with his aromatic signature never ceases to amaze me. If he was wearing pants, which he doesn't by the way, I would have to check them regularly. He is definitely a window dropper in the truck!

So, now that we have that out of the way, we can now focus on Butch's other end and examine his belching. It's really not that bad but it is another funny trait of his. There is nothing different or spectacular about Butch's belching except that after he does so, it almost looks as if he is smiling. He could be lying on his side or in his famous chewing posture but every time I hear him burp we look at each other and it appears that he is smiling, like he just ate the cat. About the only time he doesn't do this is when he is too busy eating something. Now if I could only teach him to belch the alphabet that would be noteworthy! For the time being though I think he will just work on projection.

He also snorts and grunts like a pig! He could just be lying there and all of a sudden he snorts, for no apparent reason. This is not to be confused with the snorting sigh that happens when he is relaxed and content. This type of pig-snort is short and sharp and it could happen at any time. Sometimes he will be just standing there looking at me and snort. I don't know whether he is disgusted with me for some reason or if he even knows he is doing it. I have noticed that he will also snort when he is facing off anyone who is walking past the house, with or without a pet in-tow.

Butch has also been known to let out a kind of semi-moan grunt. This usually happens when I pick him up, either from riding in the truck with me to let him out or when I pick him up when he is sleeping on my chair and I want to sit there. It is kind of hard to describe but I could swear that it sounds very much like a child groaning when they are straining, trying to pick up something heavy or they don't want to get up in the morning. I have even heard Butch groan as he licks his paws after he eats!

Then there is the "honk." It is kind of like Felix Unger when he had a sinus attack, except Butch is much louder and it is more like a full body heave or spasm when he does it. He really gets every muscle of his body into it. It is quite an unnatural looking spectacle if you have never seen it but prevalent in these types of dogs. The first time I saw him do it, I did seem to recall that Babe used to do it also when I was a kid. For

Butch and for other dogs in the flat-faced category, this is a little more common although it can potentially happen to all dogs from time to time from what I have read and been told. Dogs with this shortened muzzle or pushed-in face are said to be *brachiocephalic*. In humans, brachiocephalic refers to large veins or arteries that are directly connected to your heart. This is obviously not the same for dogs and I'm not a doctor so I don't even want to get into how it might be related. Again, pugs, Boston terriers, bulldogs, and other short-muzzled dogs are more susceptible to this condition than others. I had a lot of trouble finding a name for it when I was trying to explain it to Butch's vet. Researching this further, I was reading additional information on Boston terriers and I ran across an explanation of this condition calling it "reverse sneezing."[1] In the article, veterinarian Jeff Werber of Century Veterinary Group in Los Angeles explained that, as the name implies, the condition is a "sucking in of air instead of blowing out during a sneeze. It is a type of snorting because of tracheal flutter that is very loose." Dr. Janice Gebe, Ph.D., was also quoted, saying that "Irritation in the throat and palette can cause noisy, spasmodic attempts at inhaling air and the dog will stand with its head and neck extended. It does not pose any real problem for the dog but it is unsettling to watch." Unsettling? If people are not aware of this behavior before purchasing a dog that is predisposed to "reverse sneezing," they really might think that the dog is choking or actually dying from something! The article also gave a few ways to help the dog end this uncontrollable action, like lightly stoking the throat to trigger the dog to swallow, pinching his nose shut for a few seconds, or even blowing into his nostrils to stop it. Since it is not harmful to the dog, letting the episode pass on its own and not interfering is also an option. However, there is one bit of a problem that this can cause if it starts up while the dog is eating or drinking. If this situation occurs there is the potential for something to get sucked right into the air passage and into the lungs. This can cause pneumonia, which could be fatal, so it is in the best interest of the dog to help stop the "honking" as soon as possible. The methods for stopping it were less than desirable for me as I did try each of them with little luck. Every time I tried to stop it, Butch would just pull and try to walk away causing him more stress. I would just have to bear with it until it subsided.

It wasn't until I was on one of my famous runs to the pet store that I ran into a real nice older lady who worked with a local animal shelter who wanted to pet Butch. As she was petting him she was explaining to me that she had owned a pug and it was twelve years old. Just then Butch let out a honk that stopped everyone in the aisle. The lady who was petting him, without missing a word, slid her hand in front of his face, plugging his little flat nose with her flat palm. She said, "Oh Butch, you're a reverse sneezer, too!" He barely got out two honks before she helped him to stop. I said, "How did you do that so fast?" "You see," she answered, "I have owned pugs for many years and they have all done that. My current pug has been doing that for the last twelve years and I picked it up along the way to help him out. Now, if he feels it coming on he will come and find me so I can make it stop as soon as it starts for him." It was so fast and so simple that I knew this was the answer. Trying to grab his nose or blow in his face was just not going to work. She also mentioned that it is almost like the flap in their throat gets turned around and when you immediately stop their sucking in of air the flap returns to its normal position. I don't know exactly what she was talking about, anatomically, but for whatever reason, the flat palm on the flat nose works like a charm. I never thought that Butch would actually search me out for this but after the first few times I helped him stop his honking, he would actually not pull away anymore when I did approach him during an episode. He learned that I was helping him out by blocking his breathing for a split second. To me, that represents ultimate trust, which comes with time, perseverance, and love. I think he definitely knows by now that I would never intentionally hurt him and he seems to show it whenever we are together. He comes to me whenever he has a problem of some sort either out in the yard or in the house.

Another endearing trait that Butch has is the amount of slobber that he can produce at will. You wouldn't think that slobbering would produce any noise and it doesn't by itself. Butch, however, does possess a unique style and sound when slobbering due to the fact that it usually happens during game time, inside or out. Anytime he catches me on the floor or if my face is anywhere near striking distance I will most definitely be covered with slobber in short order from his unending quest to kiss me. It's not that he walks around constantly leaving a trail of slobber wherever he goes, it's just that he can summon this super power at will. Playing outside is so exciting to him that only a couple throws of the tennis ball will produce a fuzz-matted, juice filled, green, soggy, lump of a ball. He can easily cover his entire body from head to toe with slobber during one of his famous giant ball sessions out in the yard which definitely makes Butch a candidate for *America's Funniest Home Videos.*

He is a real man's dog. Snoring, snorting, honking, belching, slobbering, and flatulence are an impressive collection of talents for such a small package. Even the most accomplished collegiate men in these areas would be hard-pressed to keep up with Butch's unequaled performance in just one. Nevertheless, I wouldn't trade Butch for anything in the world. He is cute, funny, sometimes stinky, but truly a best friend, willing to accept *me* with all my faults.

1. King, Marcia. *Dog Fancy Magazine's Popular Dog Series.* "Boston Terriers." Vol. 26 (2003): p. 53.

CHAPTER 17

Yard Work, Hoses, and Sprinklers

Long gone are the days of partying until 4:00 a.m., golfing every other day, and general carousing. Those days are behind me now and it doesn't bother me a bit. I've taken to more peaceful, more productive, pastimes, one of which is working outside on and around the house. Mowing the lawn, planting, and trimming are the call of the wild for me now. That's not to say that I don't like to have a few beers while mowing the lawn on the tractor. This should explain all the missed grass and crooked lines in my yard every Friday evening. I know the neighbors have wondered. I don't really drink very often either so it don't take much to help me miss a few turns with the tractor and take out a corner of the garden or flower patch.

Due to the unpredictable weather we have here in Ohio for much of the year, I could say that working outside or even just *being* outside is a pleasure unto itself. Our winters here can linger easily sometimes into May or just turn to a gray, rainy, sloppy mess for weeks on end, making it impossible to enjoy the outdoors.

Butch loves being outside and usually thinks that doing so means we will be playing every minute. Every time I go outside to mow the lawn, I put his Invisible Fence collar on him and he follows me out. He grabs his Frisbee or a ball and runs right beside me, hitting me with it or dropping the ball and picking it up expecting me to get it. When I say "OK, I have to mow the lawn now," he spits out whatever he has in his mouth and either grabs my pant leg or the tongue of my shoe and growls like that little dog on the commercials that chases the mailman. Butch has already torn out the tongues from two old pairs of shoes doing this. I know the neighbors have to think it's a scream when I walk toward my shed with Butch at the end of my leg. It never fails! When I say, "Time to mow the lawn," he drops what he is doing and latches on to my pants, growls, and thrashes his head as I drag him across the yard. He is like that little comedy dog you see tugging on the guy's pants while the man tries to carry something heavy. The only problem is that Butch is like a cement block with legs, all muscle. He has no problem pulling one of my legs right out from under me if he pulls just the right way … and he knows it. When I am wearing shorts, it does frustrate him so he will start ramming my ankles with his head! I have created a monster. He now knows what it means when I am heading toward the shed and he does not like the fact that I am not outside to play with him. Trying to divert his attention away from me, I'll throw his giant ball into the yard and he goes crazy chasing after it, trying to pop it. If he hits it past his line he will come and get me so I can go *fetch it* for him.

As I drive the tractor around the yard he usually will check things out and walk around the outside of the house if he is not playing with the ball. When he gets tired of either, he will just lie down in the garage and stare at me until I get off the mower to bag some grass or get another drink for myself.

Working around the yard, doing various tasks that do not include mowing, means that Butch will not be far away, stalking me. We have what has turned into a contest. I try to get done doing outside work, and Butch tries to steal everything from the broom, rake, or shovel, dragging them by the handle and running away, to actually jumping up and taking the glove right off my hand. Once he gets the glove, that's it. I will not get it back unless he wants to let me have it. I can try to entice him with a treat or another object that I know he likes but he is often so quick that he can drop the glove, grab the treat and get the glove and be on his way before I can get to it. When I finally have won the prize what I am rewarded with is a slobber-soaked shredded remnant of what used to be a glove. Then just when my attention is on what he has done to the glove from my right hand he often is able to run up my leg and snatch the left one. I know he has to be laughing at me just by the look on his face.

After the lawn is mowed and the other miscellaneous yard work is done Butch instinctively runs for the outside spigot near the hose reel. Many times after I am finished especially, when it is particularly dry, I will water the lawn. I'm not sure exactly at what age or at what stage of Butch's development that he decided that he liked playing in the water. It's more of an obsession than just a plain fondness. Butch has no reservations about placing his face directly in the path of a hard spraying hose or sprinkler repeatedly. City water pressure is about 50 to 60 PSI. I know for a fact that I will not even think of putting my face in front of a spraying hose. This comes from being at the wrong end of that hose as a kid getting a drink of water with some jokester controlling the water flow. Most of the time, Butch is so slobbered up from playing with the ball while I am mowing that he needs a good spraying off and a quick bath before I will let him go back into the house. This is why I usually go for the hose after I am finished, even when I'm not watering the lawn. Every time I start spraying the hose, he goes into a wild barking jumping frenzy. I know he is thirsty because nothing that small could put out so much slobber without looking like a shriveled prune. Knowing that he is thirsty, I will usually spray the hose for a few minutes so he does not drink the water that has been sitting inside the hose for a week. Once it runs cold I will bend down and barely squeeze the nozzle to let a manageable stream flow out for him to drink – he really goes to town without letting a drop fall to the ground. Admittedly, often being on the giving end of my share of pranks, I have been trembling with temptation to let him have it. As God is my witness, in that close situation, I have never done it to him. Set aside the fact that since he is so small I could literally spray it right into his lungs with that kind of force behind the water and he could develop pneumonia or something, it could also hurt his eyes or cause him to fall onto the cement and really get hurt. Yes, I have thought about this and these things would be bad enough but the most damaging thing that would happen would be the betrayal of trust that would result from one stupid action on my part. This is the most important reason that I have been able to restrain my tomfoolery where Butch is concerned, unless I know that *he* knows that we are just playing.

Once Butch has had his fill of water, the game is on. I start spraying the hose and moving it from side to side slowing it enough to let him catch the stream and sometimes spraying his whole body to rinse off the slobber and soap that I have just washed him with. It never fails, no matter how I try to keep the stream off of his face, he goes for it, face first, with his cheeks spreading out like a little parachute. Sometimes he hacks and coughs but he just keeps coming back for more. It wasn't long before I realized that he would not stop unless I put a stop to the action and the parent in me had to kick in and end it. No matter what kind of experience he has in that water, time after time, Butch still goes through the same ritual, jumping, diving, and rolling through the sprinkler, taking face-fulls of water, becoming a little water-logged over-hydrated bundle of fun. His over-zealous taste for water adventure often ends up with a potty break every two hours all night long with doggy diarrhea! Most of the time, as a puppy, he was able to wake me in time to get him outside in the middle of the night. Other times I was not so lucky, waking up to a peculiar smell that only took one wrong step to recognize. Now that Butch is an adult, he handles his bladder and water intake much better. I'm sure that after a few bouts with this problem, through repetition he may have put two and two together. It may be that he is now older, a little wiser, and his bladder is much bigger than it was. It could also be that on really hot days his little muscular body processes that water much faster and he is able to get rid of most of it during his normal evening breaks. What ever the case, he definitely has a serious opinion about the sprinkler and prods me to put it out every time we go outside.

There are a few options as to how the weather changes in Ohio from season to season but I think the most grueling is the transition from fall to winter. Sometimes we can go from summer type weather directly to freezing cold and snowing within a day or two in late October and November. As the weather turns cold, it is no surprise when it starts snowing, living as close to the snow-belt as we do. It could snow literally within minutes of a sunny sky. Snow is a funny thing for us here during this time of year. This made it quite amusing to watch Butch trying to figure out what was going on and what this white stuff was all over his yard. In general, dogs react differently to snow. Some dogs love it, some hate it. There are the dogs that don't like it, which are generally the tiny little trembling dogs that shiver in the middle of summer in 90 degree heat. They are the ones that tippy-toe out into the cold to try and do their business. Then, there are the other dogs that are looking for trouble at any time of year. Those are the ones that run head first into a pile of snow, rolling around in it, throwing snow everywhere.

I'm not sure what to think of it yet but Butch is one of those dogs that love it. The first time Butch saw it snowing outside he ran and jumped up trying to catch some of the flakes. That is until he got a little older and decided that he was too cool to act like a little pup about it. Looking through the window after letting him outside, I have caught him running around the backyard jumping up to catch snow but I never told him about it because he would be embarrassed. So it is safe to say that Butch likes the snow.

When Butch was about two and a half years old, it was the middle of winter and we had about fourteen inches of snow on the ground after a multi-day storm. After I had cleared the driveway and walks with the snow blower, I would always let Butch out to do his business and check things out. I would clear a nice sized spot on the lawn so he could sniff the earth and relieve himself in that spot. Being a short-hair dog, he doesn't have much insulation and he does not have much of a snout to warm the air that he breaths in so, as I mentioned earlier, I cannot keep him outside for too long. The real trick is getting him to come back in. As soon as he saw all that snow on the ground, he tore off running into the middle of the yard, snow flying, hopping through a foot of snow with each bound. He would run, or hop, from one end of the yard to the other as fast as he could. Stopping only to dig a quick hole and burrow underneath the snow until it would collapse behind him. Then he would try to push his way through the mound and finally pop his head up through the snow to see where he was. Sometimes, if I couldn't find him for a couple of minutes, I would look out over the yard and there would be a plume of snow flying in the air from his digging through it. If I called him, he would stop for a moment, with his two little black ears poking up over the edge of the snow bank he had made, and then the snow would start flying again. It's as if he was telling me, "Don't bother me right now I have work to do!" It doesn't matter how much he is shivering or how cold it is out there, he wants to stay out and play. I would make a few snowballs to get him to come to me, so we could play fetch. I would throw them across the yard and into the snow as he chased them. Once he arrived at the hole it made where it had entered the snow, he would sniff around and dig but was perplexed as to where the ball went. He would stand there and bark with his head tilted to one side.

At one point, when he was about a year old, seeing how he was shivering in the cold, I bought him one of those little dog coats. Not one of the little sissy ones but a nice lumberjack plaid-colored coat for manly men that would keep him warm while he ran around outside. I'm not sure which kept him warmer, the nice little coat, or the energy he exerted as he wiggled out of it and ripped it to shreds. He probably had it on all of ninety seconds. He is not very fashion conscience. He's more of the rough and tumble type that likes to bark and attack the snow shovel or the broom. A doggie coat just gets in his way. He will look for anything to do outside in the snow even to the point of chomping on the growing mound of snow in front of the shovel or running through the snow blower's cloud.

Whether it's because we are cooped up in the house during the winter, or he just likes to be outside with me, I'm not sure. I only know that I get a good laugh from watching Butch just being Butch! Judging from the good time he seems to have in any weather, I would say that Butch is an outdoor sportsman.

CHAPTER 18

Butch Country

Butch has a very full schedule. He is swamped with activity every day. Although he does like to sleep in and is hard to get out of bed (*my bed!*) in the morning, he will get up to see me off and take a quick spritz before he goes right back in the house into *my bed* and continues his beauty sleep while I go off to work. It has taken some time for Butch to learn the ropes of having the run of the house without eating furniture, wood work, and carpet but now that he knows the routine, I never find any unpleasant surprises when I come home for lunch to let him out to play for a little while. The routine now varies in that I could either leave him home or take him to Dad's to play on any given day. If I take him to Dad's house, Butch is usually excited to go if I say "Let's go see Buttons and Bosco!" If I take him over there more than three days in a row, he is usually reluctant to get out of bed and gets cranky. He is not a "morning dog." Just like I was at his age (in dog years). I hated to get up early in the morning also, so I think it is funny and even cute the way he grunts and groans when I try to get him to wake up in the morning. I know he is always exhausted when he comes home from running around with Bosco all day. This is not a bad thing as it does afford me the opportunity to do some additional work on whatever project is the flavor of the month, while Butch snuggles up next to me and drifts off to sleep. The best scenario is taking him to play with Bosco twice a week and leaving Butch home every other day to sleep all day. He enjoys his time at home now and does not get stressed when I am not with him. There was a time, however, when I would have to put him in his room after letting him out for a quick lunch break or face a torn-up carpet or one side of the couch moved into the middle of the room with a little torn trim. Undoubtedly I was upset about the torn trim but I was also amazed that he was strong enough to drag one end of the couch, which has two recliners built in, into the middle of the floor. That thing is heavy! This naturally landed him in his cage with my famous "What did you do?" statement, which sends him, head held low, slowly walking the death march to his cage, where he is imprisoned for an hour or so for his "crimes against upholstery."

You see, I came to realize that when Butch and I play outside for any period of time he really enjoys it and is very happy when he is running, jumping, and catching the Frisbee or ball and getting tasty treats every time he brings it back to me. Naturally, this is what dogs do and most dogs really "learn" to love it as Butch has. The only problem is that I have to go back to work and the game always ends too soon for Butch, which leaves this heaping pile of energy in a quandary when I put him back into the house for the rest of the day. He was quite upset about the situation and subsequently took out his frustration on the nearest thing that he *knows* will get my goat. Maybe this is giving him too much credit, or humanizing him a bit too much, but I think he *knows* to go for the old beat-up couch to get my attention when I get home. It is the first thing I see when coming in the door. He has not touched another piece of the more expensive furniture in any other part of the house – only that couch. This could be part of the reason he has developed such a muscular upper body and this, added to his low center of gravity, gives him the leverage to pull that couch out when he gets mad. This could be why Butch is so buff! Maybe I could get him into the furniture moving business!

Another part of Butch's busy schedule is to make sure he keeps close tabs on his property. Butch, being a male dog, likes to "mark" or pee on as many things as possible to let other "beings" know that they are in Butch Country! He methodically tours the yard smelling for things that he can splash with his own personal rinse, tagging anything that is or is not nailed down. Luckily this behavior has not moved into the house and I think that the reason it has not is that I have firmly placed myself at the head of our "pack" and have corrected him when

I have caught him starting to pee in *my* domain. My scent is all over the house so he is comfortable knowing that I rule the roost and he will have to spend time in "lock-up" if he tries to put his mark on anything that's mine. No, I did not pee all over everything in my house but he does know it's all mine. Outside, he has free rein so he limits his *signature* activity to the great outdoors. Now that he knows this, it is no surprise to most people when they walk past our yard that they will be greeted with a stare or a threatening bark. This includes the mailman whom Butch tried to claim in no uncertain terms when he was just getting to know him.

One sunny Saturday afternoon when Butch was just about one year old Bill, the mailman, came to the door. He had a package that I needed to sign for. He rang the doorbell and Butch erupted into his normal snarling, barking fit until I came to answer the door. Butch had known Bill for months by this time and had taken a liking to him. Bill always brings Butch a biscuit and stops to pet him and say hi. Butch even got to know him well enough that he would not bark if he saw him coming from across the yard. It just so happened that this particular day Bill had on a pair of brand new ankle-high combed leather shoes. I opened the door and Butch ran out to greet him. After a couple of quick jumps Butch caught a whiff of Bill's new shoes, liked the smell, and decided that they were now his. You got it … he peed all over Bill's ankle and left shoe and then proudly trotted away. He told me it was the first day he had ever worn them! I didn't know if I should laugh or what. Bill had to laugh. We rushed to rinse off his shoe and I got out the leather shoe cleaner. We cleaned it up pretty well and I even gave him a brand new pair of socks to wear. I offered to pay for the shoes but he thought it was so funny and said they wouldn't last three months anyway with all of the walking he does, so he wouldn't take anything for them. The next time I saw Bill, when Butch and I were outside, he stopped in the street, put shower caps over his shoes then walked into the yard laughing! He said he had carried those shower caps around for weeks just waiting to see us outside again.

CHAPTER 19

Killing the Locals

Merriam-Webster's dictionary[1] defines a "terrier" as "any of various usually small energetic dogs originally used by hunters to dig for small game and engage the quarry underground or drive it out." Terriers, developed during hundreds of years of breeding, will go after small game animals and rodents by pure instinct and many of these animals live in small holes in the ground. This may explain the terrier's quick reflexes, seemingly endless consistent energy level, tenacity, and craving for tight spaces. *Terrier* is derived, as much of the English language is, from the fifteenth-century Latin *terra,* meaning earth. This is very fitting, as these dogs enjoy a good "dig" in the yard, often leaving it pock-marked like a miniature crater-laden moon landscape or a miniature battlefield with foxholes and craters from tiny bombers. Since Butch has arrived, my landscaping activities have expanded to include crater filling and the replanting of grass. I now have a nice mound of fresh topsoil behind my shed and a reserve supply of grass seed to combat these holes that mysteriously appear after Butch takes a late evening stroll through the yard for final business of the day and a quick check of his perimeter.

In the AKC, terriers are known to be bred as "earth dogs" or dogs that can "go to ground" while chasing game, and Butch is no exception to the terrier rule. He is very tenacious and persistent in his quest to do just about anything. These particular traits may even be a bit more magnified in Boston terriers due to the mix of bulldog blood coursing through his little terrier heart. Even though Boston terriers are not shown in the terrier group in the AKC shows, make no mistake about it, these dogs still show all of the signs, energy, and instinct of the terrier breed. In my opinion, the major difference in the Boston terrier versus other terriers is the short-muzzled, square head of a bulldog that sits on top of its boxed shoulders. This feature, in a well-developed Boston, gives it a much more powerful bone-crushing grip than its longer muzzled cousins. I have not seen any research on this, and I could be wrong, but I would be willing to bet that Butch's bite, once he gets something in his jaws packs more pounds per square inch than other adult terriers with long snouts of the same weight. All terriers have a strong bite and I have seen many examples of them easily supporting their own weight while hanging onto something.

However, the simple physics of the structure of the head and muscles dictates the ability and force with which they will bite down. A square-headed dog simply has more power in its jaws than a longer snouted dog of the same weight.

My first indication of Butch's terrier tendencies was during a late fall day. It was one of the first days of the year when you could actually see your breath in the air. I was outside sweeping up some leaves on my back porch. Butch was lying on a rug that I had put just inside the garage door. As I was concentrating on what I was doing, I heard that newly familiar sound of his little nails scrambling against the cement in an effort to gain some traction and get somewhere in a hurry. In the split second it took me to turn around, again, I couldn't believe what I was seeing. An adult local cat, not realizing that Butch was inside the garage just on the other side of the wall, had slowly walked into Butch's line of sight. This was not a feral cat, but someone's house cat that I had seen around the yard in the past. My yard was part of its normal rounds ... or ... at least it used to be before Butch showed up. And so the show began. Butch had captured this cat by the right rear leg and it dragged him across the yard until Butch was able to dig in and stop just short of his line. This was a larger cat so it had enough power, as it was trying to escape, to lunge past his collar line and, hearing the beep, Butch immediately let it go and came back into the garage.

Captured? More like surprised. I am in the presence of a killer. This is the biggest reason that the chipmonks have moved back in. No cats to eat them!

Butch at five months old, I'm guessing, might have weighed about nine pounds, give or take a couple. I think that Butch was just as surprised as the rabbit, because he sat there trembling with his tiny jaws clenched literally for dear life around the leg of this flailing rabbit. As I approached, I could see that he was struggling to keep a grip and it became evident as I pried his little jaws off of the leg that he had no intention of letting go, even though he did not know what his next move was going to be. It took some effort to actually try to grab his jaws to pull them apart because as much as the rabbit was flailing, Butch was trying to shake his head and instinctively break or tear its leg off. As soon as I could catch his head and my fingers touched his lower and upper teeth, I pulled slightly and Butch reluctantly obliged by releasing his first prized quarry. He jumped and barked as he watched the rabbit take off across the street. With his Invisible Fence collar on, he was decidedly and thankfully at a disadvantage, not being able to chase the apparently uninjured rabbit throughout the neighborhood. Reading his canine-predator mind, he shouted at me, "What's the matter with you? Can't you see that I had him right where I wanted him?" He then proceeded back onto the rug in the garage to pout with a mouthful of protruding rabbit hairs, his head dropped between his front paws, frog legged, with his back two legs flat out behind his body. Yes, he was pouting, as he rolled his eyes upward without moving his head, he was effectively saying, "Don't talk to me for at least sixty seconds while I gather my wits and am ready to play with you again." This was the first time that I noticed any predatory instinct in

Butch. In fact, every time we went outside for any reason, he searched the surrounding area for something he could harass. Even though he learned his boundary line, he began to actually run after rabbits that were on the fringe of the fence line. Butch would rise up and bark, running full speed at the rabbit, chasing it out of sight into the neighbor's bushes. It was comical because he knew he couldn't catch it, being so far away. This did not stop him though. He would still chastise it until it ran away, in many cases at the last second. The rabbits themselves are not stupid, either. They recognize Butch as a threat even though he cannot catch them on a flat-out sprint. A few times, I had the rare treat to watch Butch chase a rabbit that decided to run lengthwise across the yard, which at 150 feet across, is the long way to safety. It was amazing to me to see Butch right on its heals, cutting, darting, and changing direction as fast as the rabbit did until it reached the end of his domain. Once there, fearing the shock of the collar, he stopped on a dime. He was not even wearing the collar at the time but he still knew where to stop. A high-traffic area for rabbits, my yard would now frequently prove to be Butch's ready-made hunting grounds.

Squirrels are also part of Butch's *big* small game hunt. Although our yard is mainly open, we do have a few large trees that most definitely serve as squirrel apartment complexes. Two black walnut trees across the street serve as the local grocery store and gathering place for the squirrels to accumulate and gab about current events. In the fall, every day starting in October, I can hear them chewing through the hard wooden shell of the

181

not quite ripe walnuts as soon as I walk outside. This means the store is open for business. Butch, I'm sure, can hear them even in the house, as he always seems to know when they start and stop. He never fails to let me know by lying down six inches in front of the door with his head between his front paws. From this position, he stares directly at the door, seemingly trying to will it open through mental telepathy. The second I approach, he leaps to his feet to get a good start at flying out the door. When I simply walk by, he lies back down, sighs, snorts, and gets back into his posture staring at the door. He will not even look at me if I start talking to him from "command central," my recliner. He merely flips an ear in my direction without moving a muscle. Butch just knows that those darn squirrels are out there taunting him while they run through the yard burying their food and dancing around in their red maple and pine apartments, chirping obscenities at him. I always find little black walnut saplings growing in my beds and planter barrels in the spring from buried nuts that the squirrels either forgot about or didn't need over the winter. I'm sure these squirrels have discussed the moving in of Butch right next door to their apartment complex and in such close proximity to their food supply.

Butch does not like the squirrels and it's my guess that they are the nuisance tenants of the dog world. Or, maybe dogs just look at them as food or a good chasing game. In any case, Butch hates them. When we go outside and Butch sees one, which is just about every time we go outside, he starts to growl real low. I think it's funny because he actually gets mad. The vein on the back of his neck stands out and the fur on his back bristles all the way to his tail. As he begins to bark, the squirrels begin their cackling much like two neighbors carrying on an all out argument. I know they don't like Butch, because of his consistent harassment since he was a pup. Now, I can't quite make out what they are actually yelling at each other but I can hear the occasional "If I catch you in my yard again I'm going to kill you!" from Butch and the rebuttal by the squirrels of "Yeah, just try and catch us you overgrown chipmunk!" Then the occasional laugh from them, which infuriates Butch even more.

Butch's extreme dislike for these squirrels finally came to a fatal end on more than one occasion and I actually witnessed two of them. He wasn't kidding. The first time it happened Butch was not quite two years old. When the weather starts to turn nice in the spring, we usually hang-out in the garage with the door all the way open. I do this so I can lean against my Ford Ranger® truck bed and read the paper, mail, or just drink a cup of coffee and look outside. It's exactly the right height for me to rest my elbows on. This is usually where I hatch most of my bright ideas and projects, leaning against the Ranger drinking a cup of coffee. From this vantage point I have a clear view of the intersection of the streets, my driveway, and part of the front yard where the squirrels usually run from tree to tree. I also have a clear shot of the two black walnut trees across the street at the end of my driveway.

Butch usually makes a quick survey of the surrounding areas always sure to notice the squirrels across the street. He walks around slowly, sniffing out a good spot where he needs to apply a fresh coat of his personal rinse, nonchalantly glancing over at the squirrels, waiting for his opportunity. Butch covers a lot of ground inside *Butch Country*, making sure his borders are secure and sniffing for clues of interlopers. As he investigates, he passes by a design that I have in the corner of my lawn, facing both streets. It's like a raised bed with decorative brick three courses high on three sides and open to the street for viewing by car passengers and other passersby. This design in the yard is also clearly visible from my Ford Ranger portable desktop. As Butch tours the front yard, while doing his rounds, he approaches from an angle that keeps him hidden from the squirrels in the two walnut trees across the street. Well, on this particular occasion, as Butch approached the design from the south, a squirrel jumped out of the walnut tree, crossed the street into my yard, and scampered north right past where Butch was standing. In a split second, the squirrel had dropped whatever it had been holding when it met eyes with Butch and headed for the nearest tree. Before I could even get my elbows off the truck, Butch lit out after this squirrel and pounced right on it, just before it made it to the base of the tree. Having it by the neck, Butch made quick work of dispatching it with extreme prejudice right on the spot. He turned around and proudly trotted toward me, as I looked on, stunned at what I just saw. Not stunned by the dead squirrel that he had just brought back for me to play with but stunned that he was fast enough to catch an adult squirrel in a full-out sprint. This all happened so fast that I couldn't even get a word out. Not that it would have done any good because Butch is on autopilot when the instinct kicks in and he is on the run. I can't really see his face but I imagine that he has a glazed look in his eyes when killing is his business.

This concerned me. Not that Butch would kill the squirrels but that if he got hold of one that was a bit meaner, I was afraid it might catch one of Butch's big eyes in the scuffle and poke it out. What could I do? Nothing! I think the squirrels are a little dumber than the rabbits or they like living on the edge, dodging cars and risking Butch while just trying to get home from the lousy grocery store across the street. As I said, Butch hates squirrels, is faster than they are on a dead run, and will kill them if he catches them. On more than one occasion, Butch has walked up to me with brown and black squirrel fur sticking out of the sides of his mouth. Knowing that Butch was getting older, smarter, and stronger with each passing month these occasions increased as time went by.

Working outside, occasionally I would hear a commotion from one side of the house or the other. Investigating the peculiar animal noise, I knew Butch was either the source or the cause of it. I would stop what I was doing to see what the issue might be. Knowing Butch was safely in the yard, I was never in a rush to find him because I knew he was not far off. I would always find him either sitting or lying down in the shade at the base of one of the big trees, nonchalantly panting, seemingly enjoying the cool breeze. The source of the strange animal noise was revealed upon my approach to his relaxing location. Looking up in the tree, on the first branch about ten feet over my head was an adult squirrel, quite upset and chirping wildly, staring directly at Butch as he rested on the grass at the base. Butch had chased the squirrel up the tree and was just taking it easy, waiting for it to make its next move. The tree was far enough away from other trees that the squirrel was now trapped and Butch was not going to budge. He had that smile that Boston terriers have when they pant. It was hilarious to see. All I could do was laugh and walk away. The squirrel was definitely not coming down while Butch was there and Butch was not moving until he could sink his teeth into that little sucker. This would go on for hours with Butch taking occasional breaks to stretch his legs or get a drink of water, trying to lure the squirrel down for a chase. The only way it would end was if I would come and get him after I was done working or throw the big ball into the yard for him to play with. Even killing a squirrel doesn't match up to trying to pop the big ball and becoming a slobbery mess.

Another incident happened as I was outside tearing out some dead shrubs and getting the house ready for winter. Butch was nearby, watching me and generally sniffing around again, when I heard from behind me the patter of his feet hitting the lawn in a full-out run. As I turned around on my knees to see, I caught out of the corner of my right eye a rolling mass of black and brown fur and as I turned to look directly at the action I saw that Butch had caught another squirrel at the base of the telephone pole in the corner of the front yard. He had caught up to it and jumped to bite it but only caught the tail and before the squirrel could wiggle free, Butch had pinned it to the ground face down with his front paws. I yelled "Butch! Drop it!" But before I could get those three words out, he had its neck in his jaws and shook his head violently snapping the squirrel's neck. This one was a full-grown adult and was dead as a doornail by the time I arrived on the scene and forced Butch to drop it.

Butch had grown into a twenty-pound killing machine hunting anything he could find that would come into the yard.

Even chipmunks found themselves on part of his hit list. Although much faster and quicker than Butch in the short run to the nearest escape hatch (or hole in this case), Butch would nevertheless find them amusing and chase them to wherever they would run. He would trap them under the air conditioner in the backyard, behind the open fence door, and in one case right into my clothes dryer vent. Once again, on a sunny summer Saturday, as I was doing the laundry, Butch was up to his usual antics, running around the yard tugging on the clean clothes that I had just brought up to dry outside, when we both noticed, almost at the same time, a chipmunk running across the cement on the back porch. Butch naturally ran after it, chasing it into the window-well near the end of the porch. I didn't think much of it because I was putting the clothes out to dry. Noticing Butch digging in the window-well with his head and shoulders in the well and his back legs on the cement porch, with his rear end sticking up in the air, I walked over to see what he was doing. He was digging a hole near the back of the window-well. I saw a small space between the house and the well casing and thought Butch was looking for the chipmunk that had to have escaped through that crack. I said, "Come on, Butch, he got away. You won't find him." After this, for an entire week, every time I let him outside, Butch would go back to that window-well and start digging. I had to go and literally pick him up to get him to leave. Every time we went outside he went directly for that window well before he would do anything else. I couldn't understand why he would not forget about the stupid chipmunk. That is, until I started doing laundry again about ten days later. As I walked toward the dryer, I noticed a slight strange odor that I couldn't quite place. I began to think that I may have walked through one of Butch's famous flatulent minefields that he leaves around the house from time to time. I dismissed it as being just that and went about my business. Little did I know what was about to hit me as the first batch of washed clothes needed to be placed in the dryer. I opened the dryer door and the gagging stench of rotting carcass was unbelievable. It was the chipmunk that Butch had chased into the window-well almost two weeks before. That chipmunk fooled us both – well, at least it fooled me. Butch could smell it coming from the dryer vent and that's why he would not leave that window-well alone. Disassembling the dryer vent to retrieve that thing was not a pleasant experience. I immediately put a wire mesh cage over the dryer vent to prevent this from happening again.

With all of this small game in our area Butch is not the only predatory neighbor that the squirrels have to worry about. On an early fall Saturday morning I was standing at my post next to the truck, drinking my coffee, while Butch was sniffing around the edges of the driveway. As I was leafing through the newspaper I heard what sounded like a wet *plop* just out side the garage door. Butch and I looked at each other and then another soggy *slap* like something hitting the cement. I walked outside the garage and saw a chunk of some type of meat. I said, "Look Butch, it's raining meat!" Just then, the rear hind quarters of what looked like a half eaten squirrel fell from the sky and landed in the flower bed mulch next to the antenna with a *thud*. As I started to look up, Butch ran over to see what it was, and *thud,* a live squirrel hit the cement sidewalk next to where I was standing. It squealed and before Butch could pounce on it I yelled "LEAVE IT!" Surprisingly he stopped in his tracks and sat right down. I could see that the squirrel had been seriously hurt from the fall. I should mention that right outside the garage next to the mail box is our antenna tower which is one of the highest points in the neighborhood. I looked up and saw a very large owl fly off the top of the highest point causing the entire tower to rattle. His wingspan was at least six feet across and its body seemed to be about three feet long. The tower, I know, is forty feet high and the antenna is about six feet in length so I could easily estimate the size of this owl. It appeared that the sight of Butch had interrupted this owl's breakfast and two squirrels were on the menu. Nothing like stuffing yourself right before bedtime! At this point I was standing there processing why it was raining meat outside my garage door at 8 am on a nice warm fall morning. The screaming little squirrel finally brought me back to my senses and when I looked at Butch he was still sitting there obediently trembling waiting for my release command. I took a closer look at the squirrel, which had just fallen forty feet onto a concrete sidewalk. His rear legs were broken and he no doubt was bleeding internally. There was nothing I could do for it and it was suffering. I looked at Butch and said "OK, Butch." He jumped up and grabbed the squirrel snapping its neck, putting it out of its misery. As my little hit man started to trot away across the driveway. I shouted "Stop right there!" He stopped and turned to look at me with a mouthful of lifeless rodent. I said "Drop It!" in a stern low voice. He reluctantly gave up the prize that he thought was his. Looking up at me he moaned what seemed to say, "You are absolutely no fun anymore!" I had to take it from him because all he wanted to do was rip the guts out of it and find the squeaker inside. So with this latest kill his total was four and a half. I only give him half for this one since chasing a squirrel with broken rear legs is not much of a hunt. It was more of a mercy killing anyway.

We don't have roving packs of wolves where we live but with hawks, owls, and the occasional red tailed fox trotting around it truly is Butch's wild kingdom. Meat raining from the sky is not an everyday occurrence here but the occasional wild-life happening does make things a bit more exciting, especially with Butch here to protect me from the various fauna that drops unexpectedly from the sky.

The obscenities and bickering between Butch and the squirrels continue to this day. I don't think it will ever end but Butch is undeniably king of his domain. Killing anything that contests his authority, he rules his kingdom with an iron jaw.

1. *Merriam-Webster's Collegiate Dictionary,* 11th edition, "Terrier" (Springfield, MA: Merriam-Webster, 2003).

CHAPTER 20

Bombs Bursting in Air

Nothing strikes more fear in the heart of a parent than losing a child in a crowd or being home and realizing that the child is not where they thought he or she was. Much the same can be said for pets and this heart-wrenching situation became painfully, if not frantically, clear to me on the Fourth of July, when Butch was almost one year old.

Not doing much but relaxing on that holiday, which was in the middle of the week, I spent most of the day playing with Butch. We even took a short drive to the lake to walk around a bit. It was a fun day and we did a few things that we do not usually have the opportunity to do. With everyone from my family going in different directions for the day and some even having to work, I had a few friends over to grill some steaks and have a few drinks. In the middle of the summer, the sun does not set until around 8:30 or 9:00 p.m. here in Ohio. After sunset it still takes a good forty minutes for the sky to become completely dark. Dark enough for fireworks that is. Around 8:00 p.m. my guests decided to go home before the roads started to get clogged up with cars and people going to get a good seat to see the local fireworks. We said our goodbyes and they were on their way. I went back in the house to clean things up a bit and then took Butch outside to see the people walking by.

Where I live, the community has a big Fourth of July celebration. There is a parade in the morning and the local YMCA puts on a small marathon run. They follow that with a nice picnic in the park, which is located near the high school and adjacent football stadium. They have bands perform in the stadium parking lot and everyone is able to have a safe family holiday and a good time. I don't believe I have ever heard of anyone being arrested or disorderly. The day's activities culminate later in the evening, around 10:00 p.m., with the city fireworks display, which are launched from the high school football field. Living only a few blocks away, we are susceptible to the local traffic and people walking down the street toward the event. Being in such close proximity to the stadium, it is possible to easily view the fireworks right from my driveway and front yard. I have a great view, don't have to drive in the traffic, and can greet the neighbors as they walk by. Most of them stop to say hi to Butch and give him a quick pat on the head before moving along. Some of the neighbors who live close by will stop and sit in the corner of our lawn, which they are always welcome to do every year. Butch enjoys this and they like to see him also. Most of them are familiar with Butch, seeing us play in the yard through the year as they drive by.

With 10:00 p.m. approaching and the start of the fireworks, I knew that Butch would freak out once they started so I thought it would be a good time to put him in the house. Butch, for whatever reason, is terrified of loud sharp noises and the big boom from fireworks and thunder. Knowing that he was safe in the house, I went back outside to watch the display with the neighbors and talk a little. It was a nice presentation and it lasted about thirty minutes. As the fireworks ended, everyone started to scatter. The street filled up with cars leaving the festivities and people again appeared in the street, walking back home from the stadium. After gathering the chairs and putting them in the garage. I went in the house to collect Butch and bring him back outside to show him that all was well and there was nothing to be afraid of. I found him exactly where I thought he would be … in his cage, under his blanket, trembling. At the time, Butch weighed in at about fifteen pounds and he was not yet fully grown. He still had that weird shaped head that Boston terrier puppies have before they are fully developed.

Coaxing him out of the cage I picked him up and rubbed his head, trying to comfort him. Taking him outside, I wanted to show him that everything was OK and that there was nothing to be scared of. After setting him down on the driveway, he slowly looked around, still trembling, so I walked toward the backyard through the gate and he followed me. I said, "See, nothing to worry about!" Just then, we heard a distant low boom. It wasn't especially loud nor particularly frightening. Butch and I looked at each other and I looked up at the night sky to look for another flash or something, turning away for a split second. I looked back down and he was gone! I didn't even hear him leave! I went into the garage calling him … with no luck. I looked under the truck, at the base of the stairwell leading downstairs, under the shelves … everywhere. He was not there or he was a very good hider.

Before I realized how serious this situation was, I had remembered a scene from a film I saw many years ago with a woman trying to run across her lawn in a nightgown and high-heeled slippers with the pink fuzzy strap, waving her arms in the air and frantically yelling "My baby, my baby." She was looking for her kid who had run away from home. I got a chuckle out of it, as I was looking for Butch. But that chuckle quickly turned to worry as I found no Butch in any of his past hiding spots. *Oh No,* I thought as I began to feel the panic set in. *He doesn't have his collar on either!* As I ran into the front yard calling him, I was not wearing pink fuzzy high-heeled slippers, or a nightgown, but I was almost as frantic as that lady as I was looking under shrubs and in the bushes next to the house with a flashlight. I still had no luck and I really began to feel sick.

He must have panicked when he heard that boom, and bolted out of the yard! I pictured him being scared out of his mind, running as fast as he could through the neighborhood not recognizing anything and becoming more frightened with every passing second. I thought that he might be heading toward one of the main streets a couple of blocks away. I had to do something fast because with his color being so dark and it being nighttime, he would surely be hit by a car and killed if he reached Maple Street. The other possibility was that someone would pick him up and take him home since he was not wearing a collar. Since this was the Fourth of July, it meant that I would probably never see him again. People come here from all over to see the fireworks and if they pick him up, they will definitely keep him. My mind was racing with every bad possibility fueling my panicked state.

As I turned to run into the house, my neighbor, Christian, came over and asked, "What's wrong?" He could see the panicked look on my face. "Butch bolted out of the yard when he heard the fireworks in the distance and I can't find him!" I answered. "Which way did he go? I'll help you look," Chris offered. I told him, "Head toward Maple one block over and I'll get the truck!" I ran into the house and called the police department to let them know, just in case anyone would call about him. I then grabbed the keys and jumped into the truck, leaving the garage door open and all of the lights on, just in case he would come back while I was gone. I went around the block and up and down the neighboring street calling "Butch, here buddy!" and whistling until my mouth was so dry I could barely call him anymore. I thought, *I'll go get one of his really loud squeaker toys, he will recognize that from a distance.* As I pulled back into the garage, I took a quick look around and he was still no where to be found. I walked into the house to get one of the loud squeaker toys and I had that heart-wrenching, sinking feeling as I thought to myself, *That's it. He's gone and I'll never see him again. It's all my fault, how could I be so stupid to not have his collar on him?* I slowed down as I walked down the hallway toward Butch's room, all I could think of was how scared he must be, not knowing where he was or how to get back to the safety of home. I felt that dreadful familiar fear that a lost little boy gets in a crowd of people when he first realizes that he is lost and can't find one of his parents. I could feel myself beginning to get more upset and starting to well up inside.

I turned the hallway light on as I walked into his room glanced at the cage with nothing but a thick blanket lining the bottom and stood there staring at the toys on the floor. Trying to determine which one would be the loudest, I slowly bent down to pick a couple of them up. I began to realize that it was probably fruitless by now to even try to look any longer, after forty-five minutes of looking, and that his fate was already sealed. As I stood there dejected, staring at the toys I was holding in my hands, I thought of driving down to Maple and going around the block to see if he had been hit and was lying in the street. I knew I couldn't bear to see him like that but I had to know … and what was I going to tell my Dad?

I figured that if I was going down there, I might as well take a loud toy and squeak it and he might just hear it and be OK. I tried one squeaker but it wasn't loud enough and then I remembered the little white ball with feet. It was obnoxiously loud and he would hear this from a long distance for sure. He always responded to it. Putting the other toys back on the floor, I bent down and picked up the baseball sized white toy with feet and squeaked it a couple of times. *Squeak, squeak!* It was plenty loud enough. *Squeak!* Just then from the corner of my eye the yellow blanket inside the cage began to protrude from the front door of his cage. I squeaked it again and at this point the blanket came alive, inching its way out of the cage onto the hardwood floor closer to me. I bent down peeled back the top of the blanket and Butch poked his head out, nonchalantly grabbed the little white toy by the foot, turned around and burrowed back under the blanket as if I had rudely disturbed him while he was trying to sleep. I was speechless! I threw back the blanket, picked him up, and held him tightly. He started licking my face like we were playing, as I tried to swallow the lump in my throat. I took a few moments to gather my composure, put his collar on him, and took him outside with me to find Christian walking through the backyard toward our house.

"I found him," I said sheepishly. "Where was he?" asked Chris. "You're not going to believe it. He was in his cage under the blanket!" I exclaimed. "Oh, boy, you little knucklehead," he replied as he rubbed Butch's head. After a brief conversation and a heartfelt thank-you, we both retreated to our homes. A happy ending, a lesson learned, with me physically and emotionally drained.

I spent the next half hour or so doing some detective work while trying to figure out exactly how he got back into the house.

My house is an older home built in the early 1960s, so although it is a good solid house, there are issues of wear in some areas that are used every day. The door leading from the den to the garage is one of those areas that has built up its share of wear due to daily use. The door does not close all the way because the cylinder which closes the door without letting it slam is worn out. The door is an old style wood screen door with an interchangeable window on top and a solid painted bottom. It is a good heavy solid door and I do not want to change it to one of those cheap thin metal storm doors because of its good insulating qualities. It will close, but the cylinder is worn to the point where it will not close the door completely. It leaves about a two-inch gap unless I push it closed, once I have gone through it.

The only way that I could think of that Butch could have gotten back into the house was to mash his little head into the crack of the door so that it would open enough for him to squeeze the rest of his body through. He was plenty strong enough to do this, as he had already started to push the door open from the inside with his front paws and run outside to investigate nearby noises. This had to be it. Needless to say, I learned a very important lesson that night and that was never to put Butch into a situation where he will be too scared or where he cannot get to a familiar safe place. A side note would be to make sure he always has his collar on!

Once again, I had experienced the potential feelings of a parent that might have found themselves in a similar situation with their kids. The thought of losing Butch is traumatic to me, which forces me to take better care of him and to be alert for potential trouble. He now stays in the house when the fireworks start and I don't let him out until he rings the bell on the door because *he wants* to go outside.

Now, as soon at that first big boom kicks off the fireworks, he is jumping off the chair and running to get in his cage for the duration. Butch is safely in his crate while I am comfortably watching the fireworks in my lawn chair, sipping a cold one. I know exactly where I will find him so I can enjoy myself and not worry about what he is doing. It's safe to say that he will not be joining me on other excursions to watch fireworks. Why put him through it? I would like to have him with me but he just does not like it so I am not going to stress him out by forcing him to stay with me out there with the loud noises.

I think that I have inherited much of this nurturing attitude from my parents, which became even clearer to me one particularly bad day. It was February and I had taken a couple of days off of work to continue studying for the LSAT test, as I was considering entering law school. As I was sitting at my desk, the phone rang. "Jeff here!" I answered in my terse voice, as I usually do when I'm working. This way I don't waste a lot of time on chit-chat with people who dialed the wrong number or sales people I don't want to talk to. "Jeff, it's Dad. I don't feel very good." I could tell he was not well. He continued, "I feel real dizzy and I'm throwing up." Thinking that he could be having a heart attack or a stroke or something, I replied, "Call 9-1-1 and don't wait for me. Just go with the ambulance and I'll stop at the house and then meet you at the hospital." Thinking the worst, along with what could possibly be wrong, I dropped everything, jumped in the truck, and headed over to Dad's house as fast as I could.

As I arrived at the house, the ambulance was still in the driveway with Dad sitting up in the back. I knocked on the window and he waved as the paramedic got out and spoke to me. "He says he feels better now but I think we should still take him to the hospital. He says he is worried about his dogs." I said, "Tell him that I'll take care of them and then I'll come down to the emergency room and meet him there." I gave him the OK sign through the window. He saw me and waved.

The ambulance pulled out after the paramedic got back inside. I was relieved to see that Dad was smiling and looked like he was OK. I made a quick check of the house and Buttons and Bosco were just fine. I locked the doors and headed to the hospital. He was in the emergency room, sitting up with an oxygen mask on, talking and doing well. He told me, again, that he felt really dizzy all of a sudden and started to throw up but he didn't know why. He also said that, by the time they put him in the ambulance, he felt fine again and didn't want them to bring him in. I asked what he might have eaten but he said he didn't have an upset stomach. Then I thought, because of the way his hearing aids *shriek* when he tests to see if the batteries are working, he might have really rattled his eardrum or the small bones in his ear and it threw off his equilibrium.

The doctor came in and started asking one question after another. "Do you feel sick? Did you eat something that made you sick?" I interrupted to explain to her what he had told me and all I could get out was "He wears hearing aids and …" She then started all over again only this time talking really loud and really slow, "Do you feel sick? Did you eat something that made you sick?" As Dad tried to answer her questions he started to say, "I called my son because I needed a ride and ..." She cut in and said loudly again, "You needed a ride, is that why you called 9-1-1?" She was insinuating that the only reason that he called 911 was that he needed a ride. I had finally had enough and I stood up and asked, "Why are you talking so loud?" She replied, "You said he has hearing aids." I said "Yes I did, do you know what the purpose of a hearing aid is? He has them in his ears and he can hear you just fine." She looked at me for a second and started talking to Dad again real slowly and I interrupted again, "And another thing, why are you talking so slow. He wears hearing aids. He's not a moron." Dad got a good laugh out of that one. Although she irritated me, my sister Jeanne, who works at that hospital, said that she is quite a good doctor. I didn't care, I thought she was … less than smart.

A quick looking-over, advice to see his personal physician, and we were out of there in a couple hours. This is blazing speed for just about any emergency room. The real point of the matter was that even though Dad was having medical difficulty, he still was concerned about his daily companions, Buttons and Bosco. He really loves those dogs and they love him. The concern he showed for them, not knowing what was wrong with himself, was remarkable. It's an example of the selfless attitude that he and Mom have tried to teach us kids for many years.

The scares and the daily problems that Butch and I go through together are all part of the program. It not only creates more of a bond between us but it teaches both of us just a little more about each other. Things that we know about each other often grow out of turmoil. I understand the value of it but personally I can do without the scary parts. It's too nerve racking! Dad's visit to the doctor yielded a good check up and the discovery of a potentially serious problem. After a few tense months it turned out to be nothing and he is doing great.

CHAPTER 21

Storms

I can remember when I was about five or six years old while we lived in our house on Arlington Avenue, some of the scariest storms of all time. Well, of all time in my five years on earth! Being the youngest of four kids with an eighteen-year spread, I was pretty young when all four of us were still living at home but I do vaguely remember some items from that time frame and one of them was being afraid of the big storms that used to rumble through our area. Living in northeast Ohio, I can definitely recall some pretty wicked storms while I was growing up. I guess most little kids are afraid of storms as are some adults so this is nothing new under the sun. Noticing this trait in Butch was reminiscent of a time when I would run to the safety of Dad while in the throws of a gigantic thunderstorm.

One time in particular when I was a youngster, there was a

huge storm brewing while I was playing outside in the backyard. My sister Jeanne called me to come into the house just as it started to rain. With the radio playing, I heard that there was a severe thunderstorm warning, which at that age scared me, as it was, but then I heard the announcer say that it had been raised to a *tornado warning.* By this time I was doing OK but was confident that my sister did not know enough to be scared and she most definitely did not know what to do once a tornado broke loose. I remember hearing tapping on the windows and as I walked over to take a look out, I asked, "What's that noise?" "Hail," she said. "Hail!?" I yelled. I ran to the window and looked out to see the backyard slowly turning white with bouncing balls of hail about the size of a quarter. It was at this point that I ran downstairs to find Dad. I knew that he would know what to do in the face of this earth-ending terrifying storm, about which I was the only one who was terrified.

As I turned the corner and saw Dad sitting on the couch reading the paper, I slowed to a faked nonchalant walk. As I approached, I slowly climbed onto the couch next to him and just sat there. My sister, turning the corner at the top of the stairs, said, "What's the matter? Are you afraid of the storm?" Putting on a brave face, I said "No! Just leave me alone!" Dad, recognizing that I was scared of the storm, put his arm around me and said, "He's alright, and he can stay here with me and watch the ball game."

The issue here is that, as a mere toddler, I instinctively knew to go to Dad when I was afraid of something. Imagine my surprise when it first hit me that I was playing the role of

Butch's protector and … Dad!

I am not sure when I first noticed that Butch was afraid of storms but he definitely has a marked problem with thunder and lightning. The low large RUMMMBLING of the thunder and the loud sharp CRRRRAKKKK of the lighting are really troubling to him. Butch has always been afraid of loud sharp noises but he really starts to tremble when he hears an approaching storm. I am not a storm chaser but I am something of a weather buff. When we start having storm warnings or a storm watch I stay glued to the TV and also turn on my weather radio for the latest updates. It got to be so regular during the summer months, that Butch began to notice every time he heard that distinct-sounding computer-generated voice on the weather radio, that the loud noises would be coming soon. He would quickly go hide in his cage. It could be completely sunny outside and all I would have to do is turn on that radio and like a shot, he was in his cage for the next two hours. "Thunder phobia" I have heard it called, but let's just say loud noises in general scare him. This has been a regular occurrence since he was a tiny pup. Storms would really frighten him and as time went by he would opt for jumping on top of me while I was in my chair instead of going straight to his cage. This was a gradual turn of events as he would normally go straight to his cage and then spend less and less time there before coming back to me to hold him for reassurance.

As a storm approaches and I turn on the radio, the transformation begins. Butch will start to smack his lips as the tension builds and it dries out his mouth. He begins to tremble, slowly at first with many seconds between each shake. As the thunder increases the trembling becomes faster and his lip smacking more frequent as his cottonmouth continues to dry his tongue. He will jump in my lap and I will usually rub the tips of his ears. While I was taking Butch to training, Leslie taught us that trick. If your dog is ever stressed from an injury or otherwise, one thing that will help calm him is rubbing the tips of his ears. I have done this with him many times for many reasons and it really does work. It will slow his trembling and seems to comfort him very quickly. I even make it a point to rub his ears two or three times during the week when we are just relaxing so I can relate it to something pleasant for him. Now that he is older, he does not get quite as upset with storms, although it has taken awhile. Given the relative infrequency of real loud thunderstorms, it is no surprise that it took a few years for him to realize that there is nothing to be afraid of. Although his phobia is not completely gone, it appears as though he waits longer before he issues his internal storm alarm and evacuates to his cage. His keen hearing can pick up thunder before I can hear it and this will sometimes trigger his trembling with clear blue skies. Ten minutes later the storm arrives.

Most kids have a security blanket that they sleep with. Some have a special stuffed animal that comfort them. They use these things because somehow it makes them feel safe from the monsters under the bed, in the closet, and even from thunderstorms. They sleep easier knowing that they have this

208

particular object, thinking that it will keep them safe. I do not recall having anything like this that I carried around for safety. I vaguely remember having a sock monkey, you know a monkey made out of socks, which was a homemade job that was conspicuously placed about, but I don't recall having it for security. Butch, however, has a special security ham hock that he carries around with him to bed or when he feels scared. As soon as the first rumble of thunder happens or I turn on that weather scanner, he darts into the other room for a few seconds then reappears with his security ham hock in his mouth. This makes him look like he has a giant dark brown smile from ear to ear. Sometimes I will not see that thing for weeks but Butch knows exactly where it is at all times. Being that he does bring it to bed with him sometimes, in my bed that is, I will occasionally roll over onto it and feel this hard piercing sensation in the middle of my back, but other than that, he has a special top-secret hiding place for it that only he knows about.

It is not surprising that this little fellow has the fear of loud noises that he does, although his mother Buttons and younger brother Bosco do not seem to have this same fear. What *is* surprising to me is the lengths that I automatically go to in order to comfort him when he is being stressed out by his fear. Normal parents do not laugh at or make fun of their small children when they come to them afraid of something. They will hold and comfort them as best they can, trying to get their mind off of the fear. As soon as Butch hears the thunder start, his ears will perk up and he will look at me with those big blue and brown

209

eyes and tear off into the other room to get his security ham hock. I usually try to make sure that I am on the floor waiting for him when he returns because this means that I am ready to play ball or tug the rope with him. Playing with me on the floor is higher on his list of priorities than being afraid of a storm so this supersedes any fear that he might have. I will wrestle around with him during a bad storm tossing the ball or tugging the rope, all while the thunder is blasting around us and he is seemingly ignoring it by concentrating on what we are doing.

This is the call of duty (not doody) of a new dog dad. I didn't know that I had it in me!

CHAPTER 22

Do Dogs Go to Heaven?

This is a subject that I have thought much about since Butch came home with me for the first time. I should probably give you a little more information on my existential background and where I am coming from on this subject to relate my point of view. I come from a Catholic family and still go to church every week. Although I attended public schools, I went to Catholic Christian Doctrine or CCD classes every week throughout my grade-school years, learning the Catholic catechism until my confirmation in the eighth grade. Now, at that age, I was not much interested in the spiritual realm of existence but I thank God today that my parents pretty much made me go week in and week out even though I didn't especially want to. I was more interested in riding my bicycle, playing kick the can, and baseball than in listening to a bunch of stuff I was not *yet* interested in.

I'm not sure exactly at what point the transformation began, but I do recall going to church steadily throughout my teenage years and even into college without being told to go. When I was twelve years old, we moved to another area of the city where I was blessed with a great friend. Little did I know then that, through thick and thin, Dave would be the friend of a lifetime. To this day, we are more like brothers than many brothers I know and I am proud to call him my friend. He and his wife Judy, along with their daughters Erin and Elise, moved to Chicago a few years ago. But just like families do, we stay in touch as best we can, visiting whenever possible, which is usually never enough!

Dave, who comes from a great family, was also raised in a strictly Christian household. We were not angels growing up and we did get into our share of trouble but, all in all, we had a very good beginning in life and were best friends from pretty much the time we met. Being roommates throughout college, I was again blessed with Dave's insight and steadfast involvement with his church activities, which I was always invited to attend with him. It was in college that I picked up the habit from him of reading *Our Daily Bread*, a Christian daily devotional, every night before going to sleep as I watched him do without fail. I still read it every night after all these years. I guess it was during these years of college when I started thinking more of my spirituality and took a turn for the better rather than the worse, which is so much the case, in my opinion, on many college campuses in today's world.

It was a freezing cold February day when I was about twenty-eight years old. I was driving home from work when it hit me like a ton of bricks and I finally realized, "I get it!" I was tracking through the stations on the radio as I was driving the one-hour stretch back home and the search had stopped on one of the local religious stations. It was about 4:30 p.m. and a minister named Chuck Swindoll was being broadcast. I don't recall exactly what he was saying but a feeling came over me that I can't explain. I guess you could call it an awakening of sorts, but it seemed like I understood what he was saying with my soul and not just my brain. People call it different things such as being born again or a spiritual awakening – whatever you want to call it, I most definitely felt it. I was not a completely different person afterward nor did it change my views on many things. I think I was just more aware of everything going on around me and in my life from that time on. Whatever it was, I look back at that day in particular and see it as a gift. Perhaps it was a tap on the shoulder, God saying "I think you are ready to grow a little more now." There are many different events that occurred over a long period of time since college that led me to engineer the collection of beliefs that I now have. I think each person has their own theory on the afterlife and what that holds for individuals but I'm not sure if anyone under the age of twelve even thinks of this unless they lose a pet or loved one and begins asking serious questions. I love kids and hope to have children one day but not being around kids very often, it is hard for me to gauge how inquisitive they may or may not be regarding this subject. After all, many *adults* do not want to think about the death of a loved one ... including a beloved pet.

Last September, I was outside with Butch throwing the ball and stopping to watch him throw up all of the treats I had just given him during our game of fetch, when my neighbor Rich pulled up in his car and got out to see Butch. We were watching Butch play with his giant green ball and we started talking. He mentioned that his dog Brandi, a Bassett hound, was not doing real well and that it was getting tougher to take proper care of her. She was almost sixteen years old and he was not sure how much longer she would live. Rich is retired now and he was mentioning that it is difficult for him and his wife to go anywhere because his dog cannot get around too well on her own, is going completely blind, and is starting to have a difficult time controlling her bodily functions in the house. I have read about the symptoms of aging in dogs and for dogs that die of old age, much like us, their bodies give out long before their heart and mind do. I think this is what makes it so difficult for us to take, knowing or projecting how they must be feeling in their final hours.

I could tell that Rich was shaken up about the idea of having to put her to sleep after she had been with the family for such a long time. She was truly a part of his family. She was there when the kids grew up, went off to college, got married and started families of their own. She was the last one left at home after the nest was empty and he and his wife were once again on their own, as they were when they were newlyweds. Brandi was his constant companion and friend. As I listened to him, I watched Butch run around the yard playing. I was feeling kind of strange, almost guilty, that Butch was so full of life and here is my good friend telling me he has to put his old dog to sleep with both of us manly men welling up at the thought. I said, "You should get another one!" He replied "No, it's just too hard when they die. I couldn't take having to make the decision to have a dog put down again." I was happy to see that Butch was able to lift Rich's spirits a bit and make him laugh before he got back into his car and drove off, but the whole discussion left me with many questions about my new life with Butch that I never would have been asking before he came along.

I began wondering how Butch was aging and how old he would be when he was no longer there waiting for me to get home from work; when he was no longer there to plop right down on top of me when I was sleeping; when he was no longer there to join me for a nap in the recliner, lying between my crossed legs; when he was no longer there to sit on my feet, staring at me with a ball in his mouth while I read the paper. There are a million things that I will miss when Butch is gone and getting a new dog will not bring him back. Once I had established the ground rules for the pain of losing Butch, I wondered, once he *is* gone, would I ever see him again? To some, it might be a foolish question, but to me it is a question of eternity. Will Butch go to heaven? Oddly enough, this is something I had never thought about regarding an animal before. If I had ever heard it, I sure didn't remember nor did I pay attention to it because I never had a reason before. This may be one for the ages but I had to at least look into it for my own knowledge.

The preconceived answer in my own mind was exactly what I wanted to hear, "Of course, Butch will go to heaven and I'll see him when I get there!" This was the general attitude that I held on the subject but there was an unsettling air of doubt that surrounded the whole issue for me. I thought, "Although dogs are one of God's creations, what if He doesn't want them in heaven?" After all, I'm no expert on the Bible, but I don't recall anything in there about animals going to heaven, and the dog references that I read have not been what I would call favorable. "This is an interesting question," I thought.

I started talking with a few church-going friends about this. This led to some interesting conversations on the matter. One such conversation was with Mark, a good friend of mine at work. Mark is a good Christian fellow and is very knowledgeable on the subject of the Bible, so I thought he would be a great place to start with this question. One of the things that we discussed was that only conscious beings will go to heaven (or not). This means that only beings who know right from wrong can make the decision to act one way or the other and be fairly judged. Therefore, they can be determined by God to be acceptable to go to heaven. Well, many dogs including Butch know when they have done something wrong. Also, don't most trainers and books tell you that your dog lives to please you? I have found this to be the case with Butch. This leads me to believe that dogs have a higher degree of consciousness than many give them credit for. When I look deep into Butch's big soulful eyes as he looks at me with longing when I leave him at Dad's place or at home, I can't help but think that there is a conscious, thinking, being behind those eyes who understands more of what I say to him than I could ever know. Now, I'm no theologian, or spiritual expert, and this conversation could have gone on forever but the fact is, at this point in my understanding, only God knows His plan for the afterlife as far as animals are concerned.

Taking the search one step further, I thought that I would talk to someone that I have tremendous respect for and that might have some additional insight into the purpose of God on this topic. One Sunday after church, I spoke with Father Jay after he had mentioned that there are activities such as locally sponsored dog walks in the park where they request him to come and say an opening prayer and to even bless the dogs. I said, "I have never heard of that." He mentioned that this was the first time he had done it. I thought it was kind of peculiar but a good idea nonetheless, given this topic of study that I had recently undertaken. After some other minor chit-chat, I asked him if he thought that dogs go to heaven and this started an interesting albeit short conversation. We both agreed that there are some dogs that deserve to go to heaven before some people that are out there today and that, since dogs are one of God's creations, there is no reason that He could not bring them into heaven if He wanted to. After all He is God, it's His call. He went on to say, "Since God is the creator of all creatures, and death is the common passage of all creatures, and since St. Paul says in Romans 8:19, 'Indeed the *whole created world* eagerly awaits the revelation of the children of God,' pets in heaven, in my mind and heart, will be right there with us." I thought this was a great answer to my question, "Do dogs go to heaven?"

There was no debate over the matter if a dog has a soul but talking to another priest on the subject, he agreed that dogs do have a soul but it is not a *mortal* soul. All in all, the sum of the very short discussions that I have had with clergy has not led to a negative answer but rather a general "God is God and His will be done. If He has decided that dogs will be in heaven with us then that's the way it will be." One thing for sure is He already knows the answer and has already made it perfect whatever the case.

While continuing to search for the answer to this question, I ran across an article in a local newspaper that went into additional detail on the subject of animals and religion. This prompted me to take an additional, more in-depth, look at this question about animals. I found that on October 4 each year, there is a memorial to Saint Francis with religious services in different denominations, including Catholic, which is called The Feast of Saint Francis of Assisi, the patron saint of animals and ecology. This feast is observed by Catholic, Episcopal, Lutheran, and various Protestant denominations. St. Francis of Assisi was born in 1181 in Assisi, Umbria, Italy. He was a lover of all creation, a champion of justice, and was also the founder of the Franciscan Order of Monks.

Among many other things, he wrote the *Canticle of Creatures.*[1]

Canticle of Creatures

All praise be yours, My Lord, through all that you have made.
And first my lord Brother Sun, who brings the day ...
How beautiful is he, how radiant in all his splendor!
Of you, Most High, he bears the likeness.
All praise be yours, my Lord, through Sister Moon and Stars;
In the heavens you have made them, bright and precious and fair.
All praise be yours, my Lord, through Brothers Wind and Air
...
All praise be yours, my Lord, through Sister Water,
So useful, lowly, precious and pure.
All praise be yours, my Lord, through Brother Fire,
through whom you brighten up the night ...
All praise be yours, my Lord, through Sister Earth, our mother,
Who feeds us...and produces various fruits
With colored flowers and herbs ...
Praise and bless my Lord, and give him thanks,
And serve him with great humility.

1. *St. Francis of Assisi: Writings and Early Biographies*, edited by Marion A. Habig (Franciscan Herald Press, Chicago, 1973).

Being a writer and producer of music myself, the fact that Saint Francis was also a composer is near and dear to me. He composed songs and hymns to God and about nature. There are other denominations that bless pets but do not necessarily reference the feast. In all cases, however, there is a blessing of the pets, which naturally includes dogs. Some have full services where the owners actually bring their pets to church with them and they are blessed. Other organizations have activities such as charity walks where clergy, some of whom own pets themselves, will attend and bless the pets (and the people) before the event begins. I have found that there is even a special prayer, called the *Prayer for Animals*, that was written specifically to be prayed on this feast day.

Prayer For Animals

God our Heavenly Father, You created the world to serve humanity's needs and to lead them to You. By our own fault we have lost the beautiful relationship which we once had with all Your creation. Help us to see that by restoring our relationship with You we will also restore it with all Your creation. Give us the grace to see all animals as gifts from You and to treat them with respect, for they are Your creation. We pray for all animals who are suffering as a result of our neglect. May the order You originally established be once again restored to the whole world through the intercession of the Glorious Virgin Mary, the prayers of Saint Francis and the merits of Your Son, Our Lord Jesus Christ, Who lives and reigns with You now and forever. Amen.

At Franciscan churches, a friar with brown robe and white cord often welcomes each animal with a special prayer which may be the "Prayer for Animals" cited here. Although all denominations are slightly different and give different types of blessings, the actual *Blessing of Pets* usually goes something like this:

"Blessed are You, Lord God, maker of all living creatures. You called forth fish in the sea, birds in the air and animals on the land. You inspired St. Francis to call all of them his brothers and sisters. We ask You to bless this pet. By the power of Your love, enable it to live according to Your plan. May we always praise You for all your beauty in creation. Blessed are You, Lord our God, in all Your creatures! Amen."

It seems to me that there is an inherent religious attention to pets who are our companions during our life here on earth. There is a religious basis and responsibility for us to care for all of God's creatures, which includes dogs. This being the case, I was not too surprised to find out that the Humane Society of the United States has a whole section of their Web site dedicated to religion. It is called "Animals and Religion" and it discusses many issues related to pets and animals of all kinds. This special day each year, when there is a seemingly strange occurrence of pets and animals of all types being led to churches around the world to be blessed, answers many questions for me on the issue of dogs going to heaven. This activity, based on the writings and beliefs of Saint Francis, which have lasted more than 1,000 years (and were at least part of the reason Francis was made a saint), leads me to believe that God does love our pets as much, if not more, than we do. He is concerned about the welfare of each and every animal, each and every pet on the face of the earth. Therefore, I believe that there is a very good possibility, given the attention the church gives to the blessing of animals, that Butch will go to heaven and hopefully be there with me one day. With God all things are possible and this is enough to give us all hope that our pets will be with us again some day after they, and we, pass away.

Because this has raised many new questions in my mind, I could definitely go on further about this subject and may well continue this study in the future, but I think that it would be beyond the scope of this book, for the time being, to introduce more questions. However, there is one gnawing question that I have that I'm not sure there is any information available to answer it and that is, "What kind of dog does God have and what brand of dog food does He use?" Sorry, that's two questions! Maybe He has one of each so don't forget that dog spelled backwards is God!

CHAPTER 23

Torpedo In The Water

Looking out on one of our dreary, rainy days that   Ohio is so famous for, my mind began to wander, thinking of the warm beautiful days of the previous summer and all of the things Butch and I did together. These good times also reminded me of how fast things could go sour if I was not careful when taking him to an unfamiliar place. This is the part where I thank God that I spent the time taking him to training classes on those cold winter nights when he was a pup. I learned much more than simple training techniques from Leslie and Cheryl, so don't ever let anyone tell you that training your dog is a waste of time!

It was another sunny July day in Ohio. As it was the last day of my vacation, I thought it would be a good idea to take a road trip to Atwood Lake with Butch. I love Atwood because I had spent many summers there while growing up. I learned to swim and drive a boat as well as caught my first fish there with Dad, so the lake holds many special memories for me. My parents had bought a little cabin there when I was about 5 years old, and it had been a quiet retreat for my family and me throughout my life. They had since sold it a number of years ago at my urging, so they could use the funds to do some traveling and have some fun in their retirement years. It was always a relaxing place to decompress from the stress that piled up during the week, and I still try to get down there when I can.

Recalling the fun I had at Atwood, I had begun to wonder if I should let Butch take a crack at swimming for the first time. I figured that, since he likes to run through the sprinkler and play in the water at home, he might like to actually swim in the lake. The last time we went to Atwood the previous spring, it was still pretty cold outside and it was all I could do to keep him from jumping right in the lake.

After a nice 30-minute drive, we arrived at a secluded spot on the lake where I knew we could wade in the water with no distractions. I thought that I would hold him above the water so he could paddle, just to see if he would be able do it. Butch is a pretty healthy dog, meaning that he doesn't have much fat on him. His dogpaddling instinct aside, I was concerned that he might just sink like a rock. Just as dogs and people have very different personalities and some humans could not swim to save their own life, Butch might fall in this same category for dogs. Because he is a city dog and all, I was mindful of the possibility that, even though Butch could have the best of intentions to swim, he might not be able to. Also, at this point as a novice, I was unaware that there are actually life jackets for dogs. I mean, I know I've seen them on TV but it just went right over my head, never thinking we would be n the water anywhere!

I put his leash on him, and we walked about 50 yards along the shoreline from the truck where I removed it. I picked him up, waded into knee-deep water, and started to lower him in. I had to laugh because, the closer he got to the water, the faster his little legs were pumping! As he was paddling just the top of the water, I didn't lower him in completely so he could get used to the idea. Then, as I began to lower him in, I could see that he was not having a problem supporting himself in the water. Well, I let him go in about 2 feet of water, staying right behind him. He would walk up onto the shore, shake himself off, and jump up and down. He really seemed to like it, but after 3 or 4 trips I think he decided that he had had enough. After a brief rest, I took him out a little deeper, about chest-high on me where I knew he could not touch bottom without swimming for a few feet, and let him go. He headed straight for the shore like a torpedo. I was so impressed that he could swim so well, I failed to realize that he was running up the hill away from the water … and me! All of a sudden, I came to my senses and ran as fast as I could after him. Clomping out of the water and running up the hill with bare feet, I had that sinking feeling that I couldn't do anything about this, and he was headed in the direction of the road. In that split-second, I could see Butch's life flash before my eyes as he could easily turn into road pizza right in front of me.

I then remembered the sure-fire, never-fail way to get him to come to me. I stopped, called out "Butch" in a sharp tone, and then started counting as loud as I could ONE, TWO, THREE… Butch, being about 20 yards away by now and at the top of the hill, stopped running dead in his tracks, turned around, and without hesitating, ran right back to me!

Unbelievable!

A miracle? Maybe, but probably a trained reaction! You see, ever since Butch was a pup, I have been playing a game with him in the house and out in the yard. He would run around the yard and every time I would throw something, I would count, "One, two, three," and then throw it. Every time he started to bring something back, I would also count and then run away from him, trying to hide. When he found me, he would get a treat, a good belly scratch, or something that he really liked. Since he was 3 years old at this time, I had already done this with him hundreds of times. It was this trained reaction that we had repeated over his entire life, that kicked in and kept Butch from completely running away and literally saving his life.
He knew that, even though he did not want to go back into the water, something good was going to happen once I started counting. Adding in the fact that he may have started to get scared not recognizing his surroundings, the counting trick

saved us both a lot of pain and heartache! Read books, try different things, go to a class, but train, train, train your dog! It is never too late to start a repetative routine with your dog. Patience and daily repetition is the key to this type of trained reaction. It might seem boring at times but it is worth it and could save a life!

CHAPTER 24

A Conversation with Butch

Not many people know this, and I try to keep this a very well guarded secret, but Butch can talk. No, seriously, he can really talk. I haven't told many people about this because not only would they think that I am nuts, but once it got out, we would have the media circus that surrounds this sort of thing hovering around our front door day and night. Butch and I like our privacy, so I really had to explain to him that if he spoke to anyone but me, *ever*, someone would try to take him away. So now, even when we are alone with people that we know, he will not speak because he is afraid someone will dognap him. When just he and I are at home alone, he never shuts up. He is like the talking donkey on Shrek. No one really believes me and even my family and friends don't believe me so we are pretty safe for now. The few people that I have told ask me in a patronizing tone, "So, what do you and Butch talk about?" They really don't understand and how could I expect them to? I usually just tell them, "Oh, not much, just stuff like what we are going to have for dinner," or what the general plan is for the weekend, or even who can snore the loudest. I can't really tell them what we actually *do* talk about because I promised Butch that I wouldn't.

Butch is quite the renaissance dog. He is interested in absolutely anything and everything! He is an animal rights activist specializing in canine rights such as voting. He is very interested in government issues, his family history, and gourmet cooking. This leads to endless hours of watching TV shows ranging from the world news to the food channel. He also surfs the Internet while I am at work. This would explain the strange charges on my credit card and the mysterious packages of dog toys and treats at my door every so often.

He is also quite the horticulturalist. He knows way more than I do about lawn diseases, insect infestations in the shrubbery, and seasonal foliage problems. Just the other day, we were discussing his future and he told me that when he goes to college, he wants to be a botanist or an agricultural biologist. He really is good at organic solutions to lawn and garden problems, which usually means peeing something to death. Like my evergreen bushes. He explained that they had *spider-blight* and that they had to go, before it spread to the surrounding bushes. Good thing he caught that!

I would say that he has a healthy curiosity for a dog his age and he even looks quite intellectual while wearing his glasses and smoking jacket, smoking his pipe, and pondering the silent freeway … Wait just a minute … what am I talking about?

So, OK, if you have read this far and have actually started to believe that Butch can talk, well, you are not far off but actual words are not exactly his forte in communication, at least not while any humans are around except me. I admit that I was stretching the truth a bit about his verbalizing so eloquently but take a moment and think about it.

If your pet could actually speak to you for just *one hour*, what would it have to say to you? We have all seen those movies and TV commercials where, by motion picture digital trickery, the animal's mouth actually moves and it actually speaks in English. Real coherent sentences emanate from whatever creature they feel needs to get a point across. In the Doctor Doolittle stories, he can actually talk to the animals and he is the only human who can understand what they are saying. This is funny and cute but these animals are from zoos and in most cases are shells of former wild animals. Oh, a few pets are thrown in for good measure, a dog here or a cat there, but on the whole it's difficult to buy. Not only that but it is a movie and you are really only exposed to the possibility of talking animals for two to three hours at the most. When you have a live pet that you interact with on a daily basis, it changes your attitude somewhat regarding this talking issue.

There are many opportunities for me to put words into Butch's mouth and I talk for him all the time. I can carry on a multiple sentence conversation with him while he just stands there looking at me. There are many examples but a very good one is every time Butch wants to play and I am sitting on the recliner relaxing, he walks up with his little porcupine football in his mouth, drops it, and looks at me like he is saying, "Why are you just sitting there? Let's play or something! All you do is sit on your behind when you come home!" It is not difficult for me to picture him as another person with his own likes, dislikes, and personality, which naturally becomes the basis for endless conversations. Or it could be just be that I'm nuts. I suppose it could be a little of that also but I normally don't have to think too long to laugh about something or keep myself amused. Even the look on Butch's face is hilarious to me sometimes when he catches me by surprise. I'll also find things to give him to chew on like rolled up raw hide and when he gets it down far enough he looks just like Edwin G. Robinson smoking a cigar.

Another facet to this hypothetical dog-talking-for-one-hour scenario is the consideration of Butch's feelings on a day to day basis. Expanding on the premise that dogs have emotions, and I believe that they do, I think that Butch might have much to say about things that affect him, the same as anyone else. No doubt he would have a few choice words for me, from time to time, and I'm sure he would have some pretty good questions also. But aside from the mundane, everyday topics he might talk about, the most important things would need to be brought out quickly being that in this situation, sixty minutes is not much time. Just imagine hearing your own pet, the one that you live with day in and day out, actually speaking to you. This is not a new concept but definitely one that I think is worth a look … or listen as the case may be.

What could be on Butch's mind that he might find important. To think that he is walking around every day wanting to communicate to me but just can't verbalize must drive him crazy. Maybe this is why he jumps around so much!

- Would he ask me where he came from?

- Would he ask me why I have to leave him every day and where I go for what seems like an eternity?

- Would he ask me why he cannot chew on anything he wants?

- Would he ask me why he cannot play with his big ball all of the time, or why I don't throw the Frisbee for him to chase when he wants?

- Would he say thanks for giving him his food every day?

- Would he tell me that he really likes the potpies I make for him once each week?

• Would he tell me that he likes the weekend best because we are together all day?

• Would he ask why Buttons and Bosco live so far away?

• Would he thank me for letting him sleep in the big bed with me?

• Would he thank me for not leaving him closed up in his room anymore while I'm gone?

• Would he thank me for keeping him warm on cold winter days and cool on hot summer days?

• Would he thank me for his nightly belly scratches?

• Would he apologize that he passes gas so much and snores so loud?

• Would he ask why my food tastes so much better than his?

• Would he tell me that he has a fun life, and that I take good care of him?

• Would he tell me that he worries about me or that I work too much and don't get enough sleep?

These are all good questions and topics that he may want to talk about but I think that if he really *could* talk it would probably be something completely different than what I, as a human being, could imagine. Despite the fact that Butch communicates his feelings with every living thing around him all of the time, there are really very few things, if I were to count them, which he does communicate to me. He wants to go out or he wants to play or he wants a treat or he is tired. That's about it I suppose. He always has enough to eat, and he sleeps whenever he wants, so all in all I think he has it pretty good. I wonder if he feels the same way.

When it comes right down to it, Butch's own imagination is limited to what I can imagine for him and believe me I have enough imagination for the both of us. The way we run around the house with him barking and me yelling, you would think there was an army of people and dogs tearing up my house. We make a lot of noise together and Butch can easily distinguish between my play-yelling and my angry-yelling and probably ten levels in between. Actually, I can't remember the last time I was angry about anything that I yelled about! In addition to being able to read Butch's feelings in all of the activities that we do together, there are many times when we are watching TV that I can just tell that he wants to wear a Roman army helmet or one of those safari hats, or even a football helmet during one of our all-out football games we play together. See what I mean. I do have enough imagination for the both of us!

I guess the most important thing I would want to hear him

say is that he loves me as much as I do him. That he cares about me more than anything else and that he wants to be with me all of the time. I suppose that is what any person would like to hear every now and then from another person, let alone a dog!

Dad tells me how Butch will sit by the door for a long while after I drop him off to play with Buttons and Bosco and how every day he knows about what time I come to pick him up. He will sit by the door for about thirty minutes before I get there, waiting for me. He will ignore Buttons and Bosco and just stare out the sliding glass door. He will not even eat until I arrive. Dad will put three bowls of food down and Butch doesn't even care. At first, I thought that this could not be true but as time goes on, I can see that he sticks to me like glue when we go anywhere and he is always waiting for me to decide what we are going to do next. He is a true friend and shows it every single day. Sometimes, just sitting and watching Butch sleep or chewing on a bone can remind me that he relies on me for everything and that, so far, I don't think that I have failed him. So yes, during our sixty-minute conversation, I think that he would say that he loved me because he pretty much says this to me every day now, with just one look into his little multicolored eyes. It would be tough knowing that sixty minutes was all the time you would have to talk about things. One hour is a long time but over the lifetime of a dog it's really no time at all. What could you possibly say during that period that would last a lifetime? As the time began to wind down and the closing seconds ticked away, I know that I would say "I will always be here for you and I will always love and take care of you." I'm sure his reply would be "Yes, yes, of course, I love you, too, Dad, now, please turn the dog channel back on." Probably in a snobbish Boston accent like Charles Emerson Winchester III!

Jeff Marginean

CHAPTER 25

A Lifetime

All things being equal, I will outlive Butch by many years. This is the natural course of events. No matter what your thoughts on the matter, that's just the way it is. It makes me wonder about the attachment that people develop with their dogs. It would seem that having such a close attachment with an animal that you will outlive by such a large margin is neither wise nor healthy, leading to undeserved stress, pain, and anguish when the time comes that the separation occurs.

Now, to be sure, there are many animals that do outlive people by many years in some cases. There are documented cases of turtles and elephants living well over one hundred years, which, unless you live in the Croatian mountains and eat nothing but yogurt your whole life, they will most definitely outlive you. I personally do not have room for an elephant. I don't think we would both fit on my recliner and I don't think I could find a pooper-scooper big enough for the messes in the yard.

These notwithstanding, animals will come and go in a person's life possibly many times. There must be a reason for this attachment phenomenon somewhere in the ultimate question of man's existence in this world. For me, this used to be a rather perplexing question. For example, when I would see the pain my sister Jeanne would go through when she told me of the passing of one of her dogs, a companion that she had throughout the years, I would wonder why she puts herself through it by getting another dog? Jeanne, although being allergic to dogs since I can remember, has loved dogs and animals as much as anyone that I know. Jeanne has a caring, tender heart and she always had a close attachment to the dogs our family had in our home while we were growing up.

I remember once when Jeanne was only sixteen or seventeen years old and had just received her driver's license. She came home crying one fall night after a high school football game that she'd attended with her friends. As she was explaining to my parents what had happened, we found out through her sobbing tears that she thought that she had hit a big dog, possibly a St. Bernard or the like, that had run out into the road in front of her. It was dark and it was on a country backroad so there was no lighting except her headlights. It happened so fast there was nothing she could do. I can truly believe this because years later I hit a deer under the same conditions. I remember that she felt terrible for a long time after this incident. I was eight years old at the time. I don't recall the car being damaged that much, if at all, but I do remember my parents trying to console her for a while.

I can't remember all of the dogs that Jeanne has had throughout the years but I can say that she has had a dog or dogs for more years of her life than she has gone without them. Through good times and bad, fighting allergy problems and bad sinuses, she has always had a place in her big heart for a pet dog. She currently has three, takes great care of them, and is very attached to them all. There are many people who have more than one dog in their family and I'm quite sure that each one has a special place in its owner's heart also. Thus, my point – that humans are remarkably attached to their dogs.

Taking a closer look at my constantly growing relationship with Butch over these past three years, I can now understand more with my heart than with logic, some of the reasoning behind this attachment. Once a dog has touched your life in a very special way, you will never be the same person from that moment on. It doesn't matter what kind of dog it is or how large or small, sometimes all it takes is just one look into its eyes and you can see the consciousness there. The feeling behind the eyes is evident if you just take the time to look. Whether it is pain, sorrow, happiness, or excitement, it's there. From the time Butch was born, I have been there for him. He has known me from the beginning of his life and now I am all he knows for comfort, protection, a belly scratch, a pat on the head, for taking something out of his eye, but most of all for unconditional love. This love, that he knows is always there, is a giving of the human heart, a part of the heart that is reserved for him alone. It may be kind of unfair, in that Butch loves me with his whole heart, holding nothing back, giving himself to our partnership completely. For a dog, this is his life and his reason for living. For a human, however, this relationship, no matter how strong, is only a *part* of our larger consciousness. It is only a part of our larger, more complicated lives.

There is a certain belief that God gave all things to man. And He gave us a heart capable of loving all of the things that He has created for us. I believe that He gave us a special place in our hearts reserved for loving each of these gifts, including dogs. I think that dogs also have the capacity to love us right back. I doubt that anyone who has had a dog touch their life would argue with this fact. There are those who think of dogs as "things," mere possessions, and do not have the willingness or the capacity to love anything but themselves. These are the individuals, that you read about or see on TV, who were arrested for dog fighting, or keeping dogs in poor or even dangerous conditions. In life, as we all know, there are many reasons for these situations to develop. There are those that truly are in situations that could not be prevented and they did not know what to do about it. There are also those who have come to own a dog (or more than one), who by sheer laziness, indifference, or plain stupidity have allowed a bad situation develop. It's these individuals that I have no sympathy for. I feel that they should not have been able to own a dog in the first place. Some people can't take care of themselves, let alone take care of a dog. Some people do not have the capacity to love any other being, including a dog. I am not talking about those who are handicapped or otherwise unable to care for an animal but those who are physically able but who are more or less indifferent as to how they live and who force their dogs to live in squalor with them. After knowing the level of joy that Butch has brought to my life, it's these individuals who abuse the privilege of owning a dog that I have no respect for, nor do I have any sympathy for the penalties that they pay. In many cases, the penalty is not nearly stiff enough in my opinion.

Pets in general, but dogs more specifically, unlock a part of the human heart that many people probably do not realize is there. I never knew it existed in me before Butch came along. I feel that having a dog in your life is a kind of medicine for the human condition. It is a daily dose of forgiveness, love, and acceptance that is administered unselfishly by an eager four-legged doctor as you return home from work. Reliving the good feelings of being with your buddy on a daily basis helps you wind down. No matter how bad the day, that little face is waiting for you and only you to walk through the door and make life worth living for one more day.

During Butch's comparatively short lifetime that he will be here with me, every day is a special one, no matter how mundane or boring it may appear to be. There have been recent scientific reports on the rate at which dogs age. They now believe that dogs age at different rates based on size and breed. The old seven year rule is supposedly not the norm for all dogs.

Let's suppose, for the purpose of this example, that the seven year rule does apply for Butch. This means that mathematically, Butch ages seven years for every one year that I am alive. This means that about every 52 days, Butch ages another year physically. About every 4.3 days, Butch ages another month physically. About every 1 day, Butch ages another week physically, And about every 12 hours, Butch ages almost 3.5 days. This may help explain the attitude dogs have about being away from the one that they care about the most! Imagine having to be away from the one you love seven days for every single day you wake up. You think time flies for us? Try being a dog.

Aging at such break-neck speed can seem rather daunting when thought of in these terms. It helps me understand a little better how those little wheels turn inside Butch's head. This may also explain the seemingly rapid learning that happens when Butch picks up a new trick or when we play a new game. It could also explain the rapid time in which a strange dog may become attached to a person. Because I've known Butch from the day he was born, I can only imagine the strength of the attachment he feels toward me. In this atmosphere of fast aging, the level of trust that can be built in a short period of time is astonishing. I'm talking about going nose-to-nose with a sleeping dog, having him open his eyes, and then close them again without flinching, knowing and trusting that he will be OK and that the person will not hurt him in any way. I can do this with Butch. I have done this with him since he was six inches long, all of his life. I have been very tempted to play a joke on him now and then but I never have. The speed with which the trust can be built is slow, over time, but the speed with which that same trust can be broken can be very fast and might not be built up again in the same way or to the same extent. This is just one more lesson that I have learned while taking care of Butch, a lesson that I could not have learned any other way.

I am not suggesting that anyone go nose-to-nose with just any dog, especially children. I have done this with Butch since he came into this world and to him it is a normal thing for *me and only me* to do with him. I guarantee that he will not have this same trust with anyone else on the face of this earth, *ever*! No one will know Butch as well as I do and he will take any such advances from anyone else, including children, as a threat or a challenge and react to it probably violently. I have heard of small children being horribly bitten on the face by family dogs even though all they were trying to do was give the dog a kiss while it was sleeping. Never let a youngster do this with a dog under any circumstance!

I have to wonder about the perception of life from a dog's point of view as they age so quickly right before our eyes. They most certainly do not realize what is happening to them and they do take every day as it comes. With the new age studies being done, there are many different hypotheses about the rate at which dogs age and the lengths of their lives. Smaller dogs generally live longer than large dogs and in some cases much longer. Nonetheless they still die much sooner than humans do, all things being equal. I am glad that, God willing, I will be here for Butch's entire life from beginning to end. Although I know how difficult it will be when his time comes, I am glad that he will know me as his best friend throughout his entire life and that, hopefully, mine will be the last face he sees on this earth before the end of his lifetime here.

CHAPTER 26

Bonding

I have always been pretty close to my parents throughout my life. Since I am the youngest of four kids and the spread is eight years between me and my sister, Jeanne, I spent a number of years as the only child left to comfortably fend for myself at home. I spent many an evening after school working on little projects of my own after playing some football or doing something with my friends until dark. I was twelve years old when we moved out of the house that my brother and sisters grew up in, to a smaller home in another school district not too far away. With just Mom, Dad, and me in this smaller home I had plenty of time to do my own thing without the distractions of brother and sisters pestering me.

This made for quite a different atmosphere than it was when I was much younger and all of us lived in the same house. When

I was born, my sister Judy was going off to college. They tell me that when my parents took her to college and we began to leave, she cried and cried over me. This seemed a little strange to some after they were told that I was her little brother. Her emotional appearance left everyone thinking that I was hers! Since I was born in March, I was only five or six months old at the time and she helped Mom take care of me all summer before she went away to start her college years. I'm quite sure that I was the most beautiful baby ever born and I do believe that part of it was that she was going to miss me, but truthfully, I think that since this was her first year at Kent State University and traditionally the first time that new freshman are going to live away from home, it is a particularly emotional time to begin with. I was only more fuel for the fire at an emotional time for all at that point. After looking at my baby pictures, I know that I would not want to leave me either … just kidding. It took her friends some time to realize that I was really her brother not her son. That is kind of a special story that I'll always remember which illustrates the spread in age in our family

Nonetheless, I guess the age difference left me blessed in the unique situation that I had a second set of parents in Judy and Ron her husband, my brother-in-law, and two little brothers in their sons, my nephews Marc and Ryan. Because of the age spread with Judy and I, Marc is only six years younger than me, making him and Ryan more like little brothers than nephews.

As time marched on and I got older, going to high school and then college, things changed as they always do and I began to notice my parents, myself, and everyone else for that matter, aging. The constantly shifting of the family dynamic changed through the years also, taking attitudes, opinions, and new arrivals in the family with it. Marriages, anniversaries, new babies, new girlfriends, holidays, funerals, breakups … life, all happening with the ebb and flow of the tides. Every family goes through some type of change, of course, but life's events just seemed to carry a greater magnitude for me with every new event as I aged. Somewhere during the planning of my life, I began to take for granted that my plans could not fail. I would be married at a certain age, have a few kids, be successful, buy a house, and raise a family. Man, things really don't work out the way you plan, do they!

As I was aging, I went through the normal separation of growing away from my parents as most teenagers do, at least to some degree. However, I was never what you would call out of control. All in all, I had a pretty good relationship with my parents throughout my life but as I got older and finally left home to strike out on my own, I can honestly say that we became much better friends. I can look back now and remember many specific things about my parents that were really good. Oh sure, they made mistakes as parents and had changed through the years but they were always there. I'm sure they got better at parenting as anyone would with age and experience but nevertheless there is always a seeming "difference of opinion" on many issues in families that seems to linger over time under a thick veil of self-control, sometimes bursting forth in quite a brouhaha. Regardless of these situations, I can honestly say that I was a best friend with my parents throughout my life.

I was best friends with my Mom for years and she definitely knew that I loved her before she passed away. I could always make her laugh and I loved doing it. Dad could also make her laugh sometimes by just pulling a rubber band. He knew just when she was in the right mood and he could do something seemingly so meaningless and she would break into an uncontrollable laugh for literally twenty to thirty minutes. I'm sure they had their inside jokes but they were truly enjoying their lives together and their retirement years before she passed away. This was evident on my visits to Florida where they had a nice little condo and would winter during the cold Ohio months. They made a lot of friends and did many things together during those years. The whole situation was remarkably similar to the parents on *Seinfeld* when they were in La Boca Vista. The comparison is cliché but true and amusing.

With Mom and Dad in Florida and the rest of us doing our thing here in Ohio, many years passed with them away for the holidays. These changes left me thinking that I had missed the boat somewhere along the way. Dwindling holiday attendance due to the kids growing up and being at their girlfriend's or boyfriend's houses for dinner, along with the shifting of venue were a bit unsettling. During those years, it was difficult to feel the same excitement for the holidays that I used to as a kid. There was a distance in the family that had crept in over the years. Different faces began appearing across the holiday dinner table – faces that threw me for a loop. Now, with Mom gone, Dad is once again a welcome face at the table and the holidays seem a little better, just because he is here with us. We all miss Mom and we feel it most during that time, but having Dad here is great.

My relationship with Dad changed drastically after Mom passed and he took the reins as the patriarch of our merry little band. Steering the boat is treacherous after the death of a close loved one but it is no secret that in many families the oldest parents are the glue that bonds the rest of the clan together. This is especially true in ethnic families and I learned this in no uncertain terms, growing up in a half Romanian and half Italian household. In getting used to his new role, Dad ran into some turbulence at first. Looking back on everything, I see now that he was as steady as anyone could be under those stressful circumstances.

Once we gave Buttons to Dad and then I received Butch about a year later, there is no doubt that it changed our relationship once again. This new connection helped open communication and kept Dad moving during a time when he needed it the most. The therapeutic effect of having something that needed him to be there every day was startling. Discussions of his knowledge of dogs revealed wisdom that he had not exhibited since Babe was still walking the earth forty years ago. Reading Boston terrier books, introducing him to the local pet store, and trying new things with Butch, began to open up an entire new world of conversation for him and me that we would never have had without these little dogs. There is a closeness that we now share that would have otherwise been held under the surface.

Taking Butch over to his house two or three times each week keeps us up-to-date and gives Butch a nice visit with his mom and little brother. It gives Dad and me time to catch up and have some dinner at least once a week. While there, I can check on his mail, bills, and make sure things are in working order. All of us "kids" check in with him frequently and Judy's husband Ron does a few home repair projects for Dad from time to time. I know Dad enjoys having him there. My nephew Joe, Jeanne's son, mows the lawn and her fiancé Roy has done some occasional yard work and gardening. Everyone in the family sort of chips in when the need arises for something to be repaired, looked into, or taken care of at Dad's place.

It's nice to be there with him in the house that I grew up in. Mom's touches still abound in every room of the house and especially in the living room, which he has blocked off so the dogs cannot get in and mess anything up. I know he misses Mom, his companion for so many years, and he is under no illusions of living forever himself. Having Buttons and Bosco there with him is just as important for those of us who worry about him as it is for Dad himself. It helps to keep him from becoming depressed.

There is no dollar value or specific description of worth that anyone can put on the impact that a dog can have on a person at any age. Dogs endear themselves to each of us that will allow them. They ask for very little and some people have very little to give, yet they offer 100% of themselves.

Family is very important to a dog and they are not shy about letting anyone know it. There is a special bond that forms when a dog accepts you into its family and I guess Dad and I have been accepted into this family of four-legged relatives, for better or worse. I have often thought of what would happen to Buttons and Bosco if they outlive Dad and the only acceptable outcome I can think of is taking them myself. I don't know how I would handle three of these little balls of fire but, God willing, Dad will be around many more years and enjoy them as they all age together. I don't think I could bear to let anyone else have Buttons and I'm not sure how Bosco would fare being away from Buttons and Butch. Maybe my sister Jeanne would take one of them. Hopefully, we will not have to find out.

The dogs, always being the conversation starter, have brought us closer together. I'm sure we would have been closer anyway, given the absence of Mom, but somehow Buttons, Bosco, and Butch have managed to dissolve any potential barriers to communication that could have arisen over the course of time. They keep us talking, regardless of mood or attitude, and bring us to additional subjects that we would probably never have discussed otherwise. I think that Dad and I have become more tightly bonded due to the bonds that have developed with us, individually, with our dogs.

The bond between people and dogs is the most basic bond

there is. Communication with dogs is possible and this is illustrated by the training and commands that dogs can learn. But this most basic bond is underlined by the fact that it helps us unknowingly grow as caring people. The bond that exists between Butch and me has been an exercise in patience, perseverance, and continual learning for both of us, one that has translated into a training course for me which in turn spills over into all of the relationships that I have in my life. A wonderful side-effect of caring for these little dogs in our lives is that Dad and I both have learned a new method of effective communication, love, and mutual respect for one another that we would surely have missed. It has opened the door to a new common ground that we can both move from, into other more important areas of discussion and life. You might say our relationship has been allowed to grow further given the new ground we were given for the roots of the relationship to spread.

The value of this gift is immeasurable and I believe it stems from God's creation. His hand is in the details of the existence of everything and in our particular case, by letting Buttons, Bosco, and Butch steal our hearts as they have, He has worked *through* them, giving new opportunities and possibilities for my relationship with Dad to grow. This is truly a blessing to us both.

It is no longer possible for me to imagine a life without Butch. I feel I owe him so much already that I'm afraid I will not be able repay him. Not getting obsessive about it, I do realize that all Butch really wants is some good food, to be let outside a few times each day, and the occasional treat after a good jaunt with the big ball and, of course, to be loved in return. It's unbelievable that he gives so much and doesn't realize it! As none of us knows how long we will be in this world, I think that it is important to get the most out of each day and the relationships we have right now. Butch has helped me accomplish this in ways that I could not have achieved without him. My life and my relationships are better because of him!

Jeff Marginean

CHAPTER 27

Single Parents – I Salute You!

I think it is an understatement to say that I now have a whole new respect for the situation that single parents find themselves in. To be sure, single parenthood has been around since prehistoric times, in one form or another, although we no longer eat our young – at least not in my neighborhood! The difficulty of not having that help-mate around to help raise the kids is not something that I gave much thought to in the past. I have seen it around me, heard about it in the news, read about it in the papers, and have witnessed it with some friends and family over the years. Regardless of how the situation had occurred, the end result was one single parent taking care of one, two, or even three or more kids alone.

I am not a psychiatrist and I have not had any formal medical training but I think I can say that we are all students of human nature if we take the time to think about the world that surrounds us. My purpose for mentioning single parenthood is not to surprise anyone but to express my new found admiration for anyone that does it on their own. Managing my own schedule is burden enough without worrying about the schedules of various little bipeds having to go to school, football practice, ballet classes, soccer games, piano lessons, baseball games, after-school activities, and the seemingly endless list of things that kids do today. All of these are worthy activities and single parents are trying to nurture these interests in their children. Running wildly from one place to another to pick up or drop off and then figuring out what to do for dinner, making sure the homework is done, signing the permission slips for the field trip, making lunches, taking care of sniffles, scraped knees, and fevers, getting the baths, brushing the teeth, and getting to bed only to do it all over again the next day – I get exhausted just thinking about it.

Wanting to care for and give your kids every good opportunity is a natural, worthy cause that almost every single parent has automatically built right in. There are some bad parents out there that we are all too aware of but, generally, this is a goal of the parents that I have met that are in this situation. Not being able to deliver on some form of this goal is a source of heartbreak, frustration, and sadness for many single parents.

Being single compounds the worry that goes right along with this natural instinct to want the best for your kid(s). There can be feelings of inadequacy, failure, and even despair in some single parents who have this goal for their own kids but cannot deliver for some reason. No matter *how* they ended up as a single parent, whether male or female, they might carry some degree of guilt because they have to raise the child alone. There are people to help out in some cases – ex-spouses, mom and dad, grandma and grandpa, uncles, aunts, brothers, sisters, and maybe even cousins and friends are all part of the equation – but the fact still remains that the burden and responsibility are on a single parent. It's a daunting task and I am amazed at how well the single parents that I know can do it all while holding down a job. It's remarkable and they should be commended for it.

Admittedly, taking care of Butch is not even close to what a single parent goes through every day and he is probably looked at as nothing more than an accessory attachment by those around me who do not have dogs. I have been *chastised* in the past for even thinking of comparing Butch to a human child. But I can only say that as an outsider, with no kids of my own, Butch is the only way I can even begin to understand a small fraction of what single parents know. Everyone has their own opinion and people are entitled to think what they want about my caring attitude toward Butch, but once again he is my responsibility and I will not sacrifice his quality of life.

I think that if you have never owned a dog and talk to a person who has or does, you will find out how "real" the experience is in trying to be a responsible owner or "pet parent" of this particular member of the family.

Kids at the very least grow up and go out on their own. Dogs are generally helpless and they are in the same place with the same people for their entire lifespan, if things go as planned. This example does not include those unfortunate dogs that are abused, abandoned, or otherwise removed from their immediate home.

Even though Butch seems to get smarter by the day, he is still limited as to what he will be able to do. He will reach his limit of aptitude much sooner than a human child will, in most cases. He will remain in a certain state of childhood his whole life due to the games he learned as a puppy. These games and tricks mean much more to him than they would to a growing child because it was with these games that we built our relationship and formed our bond. He uses these games to communicate with me and others.

Bringing the ball to me every day over and over again is his way of conversing with me. This need to play every day is part of the interaction that he requires to feel that he is part of a group and is loved. Just like a baby or a child who can barely walk or talk wants to hand me a toy or a piece of candy as a show of friendship, Butch does this every day with his porcupine football. A human child will grow and learn to talk, using more complex methods to express his friendship or feelings. Although his communication methods may change a little over time, Butch will not develop in the same manner as that child and until his dying day that little football will be his biggest and best communication tool. He will use it repeatedly every day to make sure that I care about him and that he is still an important part of our pack.

Wild dogs or wolves do not play their entire lives like domesticated dogs will. We as humans inadvertently keep them in that state by constantly playing with them throughout their lives. What is play to us, however, stops being *just* play to them as it eventually turns into the only way that they know how to relate to us. We taught them to go get the ball when they were young and we never stopped this behavior. When they get older, it becomes an important means of communication for them. It tells them that everything is OK when this kind of interaction persists. If we stop that interaction, their world comes crashing down around them. They will feel neglected and can start to develop bad habits such as chewing on things when they never did before and they could develop self-destructive behavior, wounding themselves in extreme cases. It's our fault as humans when something like this happens. Getting a cute puppy for Christmas is exciting and fun but after a few months, young Rover must not be tossed aside like yesterday's broken Christmas toys, with no means of interaction with kids who are no longer interested.

There should be a test given or a more rigorous method for people to be able to own a dog, much the same way that some people should not be allowed to be parents.

Comparing Butch to a child is a stretch in many ways but there are enough similarities that I can relate the experience to raising or taking care of a child at least to a small degree. There is the dropping off at Dad's house a few times each week. I have to find somewhere for him to stay or ask someone to "dog-sit" for me if I am gone for a few days for travel. Having to take Butch to the vet for shots and check-ups, monitoring what he eats, what he plays with, and where he is at any given moment, having to give him medicine when he is sick, cleaning up his dirty little face after playing in the yard, having to clean his ears and clip his nails after giving him a bath while he fidgets around … the list is just as endless as if he were a real child. This is all part of the overlapping segment of parental responsibility and pet stewardship that is completely interchangeable. Most of the same general rules apply to Butch as they would to a child. I believe that if you treat a dog as such it will become much easier to train them. If you were to treat your dog like a kid for just one week, I'll bet there would be a huge difference in the dog's attitude.

I forget where I heard it, but I do know that it was about ten years ago. I heard that when you come out of a failed personal relationship you should get a plant. If you can keep that plant alive for one year you should get a fish. If you can keep the fish alive for one year you should get a dog. If you can raise that dog and have self-control with that dog and take care of that dog, then you are ready to enter into another real human relationship. I'm guessing this is supposed to teach you how to care for something other than yourself. I know there are parents out there who have real difficulty caring for anything (including their own kids) more than they care for themselves. I can't speak for others but I can say that caring for Butch has taught me more about myself than anything else I have ever done. He has taught me to be more patient with everything and everyone. He has taught me to be more forgiving of inconsequential mistakes that "just happen." He has taught me how to be a more responsible person and to live for something other than my own selfish wants. Most importantly, he has taught me that there are things that are more important than work and play. This one-on-one "single parenting course" that Butch teaches requires only one prerequisite – and that is the ability to love another of God's creatures more than you love yourself.

Looking outside of themselves for the sake of their children is something that good parents do on a daily basis without thinking about it. Parents trying to raise a child on their own undoubtedly have it tougher than couples, for obvious reasons. It has been my experience with Butch, if I may be so bold, that has given me a snapshot of what it takes for a single parent to raise a child alone. It is from this knowledge which I have recently obtained that I have a new-found appreciation and admiration for what a single parent must endure for the good of their child(ren). You can call it melodramatic or whatever you want but the simple truth is: single parents are as much a gift from God as the children they love. So, after not giving single parenthood much thought for many years I can now say with conviction, "Single parents, I salute you!" Doing what you know needs to be done, for your child's sake, sacrificing your own wants and needs to improve your child's quality of life when you can, and showing that child what unconditional love is, all by yourself, is a remarkable task indeed.

CHAPTER 28

A Normal Day

The first couple of years after my divorce I spent remodeling my house and working outside as much as possible. I was trying to take advantage of the therapeutic effect of some good hard work while funneling all of my frustration into some type of constructive effort. It took a good long while for me to simmer down and get back to routine of going to work and relaxing in the evening. After a couple of really nasty back surgeries for a ruptured disc, I decided that I wanted to move away. There was nothing more for me to do around here so it was time to go. I figured that once I was back on my feet again I would start making the plans for a full-out move. The company I worked for has more than one manufacturing plant down south, so that would be a good place to start looking. I work at the

Timken Company, which is a worldwide manufacturer of roller bearings and steel, with plants in many different countries and around the United States. It's a great company to work for and the people that I work with are the best at what they do. I have many friends there and have no problem calling any one of them a friend after all of the time we have spent working together.

During the time I was recuperating from my last back surgery I was toying with the idea of putting together a project with some of the old music that I had written and possibly writing some more to make a full compact disc. After all, I really didn't have much to do. I was off from work because I could barely walk, and one of my best friends, Joe Procario, kept egging me on to do it. He would say, "I know you want to leave, but put this album together first and then leave. I'll even help you if I can." I think he knew all along that I really needed something to throw myself into, in order to help my healing process as well as to move on with life.

So, with all of Joe's coercing I started writing music again, something I had not done in almost six years. During my writing process, I thought of my friends in New York, the other Joe, Joe Lagani, who I was partners with on another project years earlier and Andy Funk who Joe introduced me to and who engineered that first project. Yes, his name is Funk and he is a recording engineer! I was wondering what they were up to and since I had been married, we kind of fell out of touch for a few years. I was too embarrassed to call them and tell them that I was no longer married and thought that I would surprise them with the final product once it was finished. I know that they would have liked a phone call and would not have judged me on my split-up but I felt that I needed the solitary time to concentrate on writing and recording the project myself.

Looking back on this experience, it was at this time of my life that I probably should have bought a dog. It would have been great at that point to have the company and I would not have spent so many nights stewing over the recent turn of events in my life. I shouldn't complain too much about it because it was my writing which allowed me to wrap up the entire situation into a nice neat little package and put it behind me. The album was very experimental and I had no illusions of it being a hit or anything. I just chalked it up to being a summary of what I had gone through during that part of my life. It was a great re-introduction to the recording process that I left behind years earlier.

While I was composing the album and recording it in my small home studio, I was thinking about all of the paperwork that I needed to do, a name for my pseudo band, and the registrations I would have to fill out. Never wanting to waste any effort, I thought, *Well, it might have more credibility if it were already on a record label so why not start one.* Yeah right! That's just what I needed, more long-term headaches! So, after discussing it with Joe Procario about it at one of our favorite steak places, talking at some length and in great detail about what a bad idea it was, that's exactly what we decided to do.

Thus, Frog & Scorpion Records Corporation was born. Having had plenty of experience in the music world while growing up, I thought that it might be fun to have our own record label, despite the mountain of work that I knew was hiding around the bend. We didn't have to move at any particular rate, so we could take our time in developing what we wanted to do. After almost ten years of working in the business, we have what became a semi-nationally known label and I was accepted into The Recording Academy as a voting member for the Grammy Awards®.

I was flattered to be accepted into such a prestigious organization but with no smash hits under our belts, it was a hollow victory. It was my plan that everyone should prosper and get something out of it. It was during this time that Mom had passed away so the furthest thing from my mind was music or the label. I did not really care much about anything for a while and I decided to take a step back and take a long hard look at where I was heading and what I was doing.

I spent the next year trying to regain some focus on life, love, and direction, not really paying much attention to the life or love part! I continued to focus on my faith in God as I had done in the past, getting more involved in the Catholic church as a Eucharistic minister and an usher. Going to work at Timken every day, visiting Dad two or three times each week, and helping him rearrange his life was the norm for quite some time. Still having to deal with the monthly business of running the record label, most things came to a grinding halt while I spent time discerning the direction for the record label.

Once Dad was emotionally on his feet again and had made the transition to a life without Mom, I was anticipating returning to the fast-paced eighteen-hour days again, working days at one job and nights on the label projects with no end in sight of recovering the investment of time and money put into it. I was preparing to continue down the same dark detour I had taken for most of the last year.

It was at this time that Butch entered the picture. A fuzzy little ball dropped right into my hands, just as I was reluctantly revving up my proverbial racing-striped life. I am a firm believer that all things happen for a reason and that although I think we all have a destiny, freewill is the gift from God that allows us to fulfill our destiny. I think Butch was sent to me at that time to prevent me from heading further down that forlorn road, trying to force an outcome where there was no foreseeable direction or cooperation. Pulling back from the building of such a monumental machine is just as daunting as starting to build it. I needed Butch more than he needed me and I didn't even know it. Butch would have had no problem settling in with another family had I not been the one to get him. He is such a happy, healthy dog that he would have been just fine. It's kind of strange to think of how things would have turned out for him if he would have been sold to someone else.

Butch has proven to be the great equalizer, helping me tone down my lifestyle and pull back from the unbelievable work schedule I imposed on myself. Much to the dismay of those around me, I just stopped doing everything by myself. It wasn't that I didn't care. It was just that I found myself doing everything to make sure it was done right instead of having to answer a million questions which would have taken longer than if I just did it myself.

Call it a purging of sorts. Those that did not want to do the work fell by the wayside and over a period of time what was left was a small core around which things could be rebuilt. Butch is a huge factor when making my everyday decisions now. My concern for his quality of life baffles many of the people around me, including my family. It's this quality of life that I wish to maintain for Butch that has slowed me down to a more normal pace, which I have needed for a long time. I still do have a packed schedule and many projects colliding into one another but I always make time for Butch and his needs regardless of anyone's opinion. I now take time to pull back from everything daily, even for a little while, to spend some time with Butch, throwing the ball or wrestling on the floor. Unless there is a dire emergency, I will forestall any interruption to the time I spend relaxing and playing with him. When called on this behavior, I have challenged those to "Walk a mile in my shoes and then talk to me about it." So far, I have had no one take me up on that offer.

For many years I was the type who found it hard to say no when asked to get involved in projects, which led to my impossible schedule keeping me in the fast lane. My willingness and ability to help people would often override my better judgment. Adding way more to my list than I could possibly handle, kept me jumping from project to project, not getting paid for any of it. I'm not a greedy person but I give my time away much too liberally. Mind you, this is for projects where I truly should be paid because I am, in many cases, offering a professional service.

Being fairly paid for what I am doing to help someone out is not too much to ask but you would be surprised to see what people expect you to do for nothing or "favors" as they call them. You can't pay the gas bill on favors, pal, especially at today's prices, and I didn't sacrifice the last ten years of my life learning how to do things just so I could give them away to the general public either! Although being paid fairly may have taken some of the regret away about keeping this kind of schedule, I would just smile and keep on going while the requests kept coming. You can't put a price on wasted life!

Most of the time, I was going way too fast to enjoy any of the successes that were achieved on projects and completely missed the point of doing them in the first place. I had become so stressed out about what was next, and who I didn't want to disappoint, that I failed to enjoy the moment of achievement that each completion brought. This method of working till I drop only led to one thing and that was flat-out exhaustion. It's hard to recognize your goal or your destination if you do not look up to see where you are going once in awhile and keep that dream in sight. With so many people pulling me in so many different directions, I began to realize that it is possible to work and run so far so fast that when you do take time to look up you don't know where you are or how you got there. This is where I found myself. I was so tired all of the time that I didn't even know what the original goal was any more nor did I care. I found out that it is possible to work so hard, and get nowhere in the process, that you don't even know your own hopes and dreams any longer. This was a pretty bad state of affairs for me.

I am happy to say that at this point I have toned my schedule down nicely and Butch is largely the reason why. Because of the routine that Butch and I have built for ourselves, I am more relaxed for longer periods of time, I don't get stressed out if things do not get finished when I thought they would, and I have no problem looking people squarely in the eye and saying, "I'm sorry, but no, I can't help you right now." I don't lose a wink of sleep over it either. I can only do what I can do on any given day and it's just tough bananas if people don't like it! I do keep myself extremely busy and I do have many music projects in line to produce but they will get done when they are ready to be done and not a minute sooner.

Even while writing this book, I had to put it on hold to produce a series of talent shows being held for a charity. They were medium-sized events but they were on a time schedule so I happily volunteered to help when I was asked to join the team. See my point? This book was put on hold for a couple of months but it got finished in its own time as you can plainly see

… or read!

Butch is my "mini-me"! He watches out for me, he protects me from the vicious neighbors and squirrels and he worries about me. If I get caught up in my work and forget the time, he will come marching back to my office, get up on his hind legs, and scratch at my leg. It's as if he's saying, "Hey, it's past midnight now. That's enough. Go to bed." I am usually so wiped out that I can actually hear him say that! A normal day for me has changed drastically since Butch arrived and I am definitely healthier now that it has. I have read that having a dog is therapeutic from the standpoint that it relieves stress, especially while sitting and petting him. I think that this is true but it fails to recognize that having a dog will change your life in so many other good ways that they are difficult to count.

The beauty of it is that the good effects can be felt on both sides of this relationship. The appreciation and gratitude that Butch and I have for each other is communicated every day. My normal days have changed into a new normal that is much better than the old. Butch has raised the bar and challenged me to live a better quality of life. He made me understand that the only one preventing me from living better was … in fact … me!

CHAPTER 29

Flashbacks

I grew up in a nice neighborhood, like many kids my age, during a relatively good time in history. Aside from the fear of the Vietnam war in the late 1960s-early 1970s, things were pretty good for kids at the ripe old age of seven or eight. Playing ball, going to school, and staying up late on weekends until almost 11:30 p.m. (wow!) were all part of the trail that was blazed for me by my brother and sisters. Making life my own by that time was a pleasure and I have some really funny memories about the things I did growing up. The house that I grew up in was an older home built sometime in the 1920s, kind of like the house that Ralphie from *A Christmas Story* grew up in, except bigger. It was a large two-story home with a big separate two-car garage. It had a small backyard and a steep bank divided by concrete steps leading to the street. It even had a decent concrete driveway leading to the back garage but it was too narrow and a pretty tight squeeze for the big cars of that era so it was rarely used except for cover during a good snowball fight. The yard was small by my standards today but I never gave it a thought as a kid. It was plenty big enough to play games and do kid stuff.

The house was situated right across the street from Lowell Reformed Church in such a manner that if you looked out our front door during the summer months you could see right up the center aisle to the altar when they opened the front doors to the church during services. This was ideal for a kid of four or five years old to bolt out the front door in his underwear and jump up and down while the people were walking out of church. This, in turn, led to some interesting contests between my parents and me as they frantically ran after me to pull me back into the house. Through the years, as the church added on, additional shenanigans were possible, like turning the big spotlight around that illuminated the large cross and lighting up the chosen house of the evening on any given hot summer night. Then watching to see which parent would emerge from the house to turn the light back around again.

I can even remember that there was a manhole cover right in front of the house that the road used to crumble around and cause a bigger pothole. This led to many sleepless nights and many phone calls to the street department for repairs, because passing cars would make quite a noise, a loud double *thump,* waking everyone up in the middle of the night, when they hit that pothole.

I can also remember mowing the lawn at that house and watching Babe walk around the small yard to avoid the grass spitting from the mower chute. I have many good memories of hot summer nights sitting on the back porch with Babe or trying to catch nightcrawlers while Babe would stomp around me scaring them back into their holes before I could catch them. Even running around the yard catching lightning bugs was a great way to pass the time for my friends and me at that time.

Winter was also fun, making snow forts for an ambush, having mass snowball wars that encompassed a couple dozen kids and two whole city blocks, and running through backyards and between houses. Loading up our sleds with hundreds of snowballs for ammunition and dragging them around the block to levy a fierce attack on the other team all the while hoping school would be cancelled the next day, which it rarely was. It's not like today when school is seemingly cancelled on a threat of a flake or two. There had to be what seemed like four feet of snow on the ground before they would even consider a cancellation at that time and even then we never found out until we got to school that they cancelled it for the day. And yes, I had to walk thirty miles to school uphill both ways in bare feet with no coat in forty-below-zero weather. In reality though, it was only a ten minute walk and when the weather was bad, I did get a ride, so all in all it was not so bad.

I have one particularly great memory when I was about eleven years old, a memory of being in the backyard just after dark on a cold winter evening. There was a good three feet of snow on the ground and more was coming down fast. It was almost a white-out condition and I was just active enough, running around the backyard and playing in the snow, to not be too cold. Mom was inside cooking dinner, spaghetti, my absolute favorite. Being Italian, she made the best pasta around and I loved it. Surprisingly, she told me that she did not know how to cook much of anything when she married Dad. She had started to learn after they were married. Well, that was before I existed so as far as I am concerned she always knew how to make things taste great! It was dark outside, about 5:30 or 6:00 p.m., and Dad had not yet come home from work. I was digging around in the snow near our driveway and Mom came out on the newly shoveled backporch (which I had shoveled by the way) to tell me that she just heard on the radio that "school has been cancelled tomorrow," which meant a great night for me and a nice long weekend ahead. As she stood there, I can remember joking around with her by throwing a few small snowballs that landed near her feet spraying some snow on her ankles. I used to joke around with her all the time and we had many a good laugh together.

After she had gone back inside, I can remember standing there in the yard, thigh deep in snow, pausing to look at the windows of the kitchen, which had steamed up to the point that they were opaque. At that moment, I can remember having a terrific feeling wash over me like warm water. When I think of it now it's almost like I'm watching it happen in a scene from a movie.

Dad pulled into the driveway in that gargantuan maroon Dodge Polara station wagon. That thing was a tank. It was so big that it would not fit through the driveway toward the front of the house but had no trouble at all barreling through the deep snow in the alley at the rear of the house. He got out of the car carrying his usual sack of change and newspaper, yelling and laughing as we had a brief snowball exchange on his way to the back door. After Dad went into the house, I knew what would follow any second … Mom's familiar tapping on the kitchen window above the snow-covered sandbox. This was my signal that dinner was ready and I had to go inside to eat. Dinner was great but tonight it was particularly good. The rest of that evening was great, and knowing that I didn't have any homework, I could settle in on whatever game or project I had going on at the time. This was one of the best days of my life. I know it might not sound like much to most people, but at that age, on that evening, for some strange reason, everything for me just seemed to be in its proper place at that exact moment in time. The universe was properly aligned and life was good. The only thing that could have made it better was if Babe had been there. She was already gone by that time.

I have had other good memories of growing up but for some odd reason this one sticks out far above and beyond anything else. I'm not sure why and I don't recall any particular reason that made it so special to me. Maybe it was the pause I took to stare at the steamed-up kitchen window to soak it all in. Maybe it was the picture of Mom standing on the backporch in her cooking apron and slippers with all of that snow outside. Maybe in some weird way something touched me at that exact moment in time that I would not understand until I was much older, an anticipation of how special that one point in time would be to me later in life. I guess that it might be a benchmark of happiness that I have compared everything else to throughout my life without even knowing it.

Although there were many great times, there were also some bad ones too. One involved being on the wrong end of a dog bite on a cloudy Sunday afternoon. Mom and Dad had gone bowling and I was left home with my older sister Jeanne watching me. After not having any luck scaring up a football game with my friends in the neighborhood, I asked my sister if could go across the street and ask one of the older kids who lived a few houses down if he wanted to play football. After a brief argument while she was on the phone, at that age we were always yelling at each other, she complied and I walked across the street and down to the house. I walked up the steps and knocked on the door and his big sister answered. She told me that he was not in the house but he might be in their backyard. I don't recall the kid's name, he was a few years older than me and new to the neighborhood so I didn't know him very well. I wouldn't have even gone over to ask but since he was the new kid, I thought I would try to make friends. I remember walking around the side of the house leading to the backyard and when I reached the corner of the house a giant ball of hair, teeth, and paws jumped at me and sank those teeth in, ripping my sweatshirt and skin open from the bottom of my breastbone almost down to my belly button. As I went backwards falling down, I can remember punching this huge beast with my fists right in the eyes, which made him back off of me. Teeth, blood, and hair were flying everywhere.

The dog was tethered and knowing what I know now about dogs, it was not a mean dog. I think I must have startled it and being unfamiliar with me and in a new home, it probably thought that I was intruding on its space. Nevertheless, I did punch it pretty hard. This was a big dog. It was as tall as me on its hind legs. It was an adult Old English sheepdog, the type with all of the fluffy hair covering its eyes that they use to guard sheep … duh! Jumping up I began to run home, blood soaked, shredded sweatshirt and all.

I recall the girl coming out on the front porch to see what was going on and calling after me to come back. I made a beeline right for my house. As I ran in the door, my sister freaked out, "Oh my gosh, what happened," she yelled as she dropped the phone. After a series of quick phone calls, a clean up of the wound, and a visit back to the same house to see if the dog had rabies or anything, my parents arrived home along with my older sister Judy. I think Jeanne was just scared and called whomever she could think of at the time. I spent the next few hours in the hospital emergency room getting stitches and being treated. Luckily the dog did not have rabies and I came to learn later that it was a really nice dog and we eventually made friends.

There are some people, I'm sure, who have experienced

similar traumatic events with dogs that happened to them when they were young. They have carried scars, emotional as well as physical, through life with them fueling their fear, as they got older. I don't know if it is right or wrong to carry this fear but I do know that I had no ill effects from the incident. I did not hate dogs from that point on and I do not recall being afraid of them either. I think I have been a little more cautious around the bigger ones after that day and I did learn from the experience, but the emotional mark it left did not last long, which is more than I can say for the eight-inch long scar on my chest and stomach, a scar that came with me through life as a reminder of that cloudy Sunday afternoon of my youth.

Like the scar on my stomach, over so many years, memories both good and bad will fade away. It's funny how we seldom recognize when these memories are happening. And this can be said now more than ever considering the speed that life seems to pass us by with in these modern times.

I am lucky and I would even say blessed to be able to recall my good memories with such vivid detail. For me, it is easy to immerse myself from time to time in beautiful memories of my childhood. I can smell Mom's great cooking, feel her warm touch on my face, and recall playing catch with Dad after he came home from work. Memories are being made every day. There are still good ones and bad ones. Most of the every day mundane memories are forgettable, but I know in the coming years, when I look back, I will remember this short amount of time that Butch and I have together and appreciate the best memories we made for the rest of my life.

For the time being though …

CHAPTER 30

Change

Colors of the seasons, growing children, friends, and relatives you haven't seen in a long time. All of these things and many others are obvious examples of "change." There are other things though, which are not so obvious, that also change. An individual life, an attitude, a heart, even a mind, and dare I say a soul are all real and are also things that can change. We all possess these things and yet no matter how hard we try to control them, we come to realize that we cannot control even the smallest part of any one of them. The certainty of change is unstoppable, seemingly moving within and all around us at its own constant will. The passing of the old to make room for the new is the natural order of life and yet it is something that can cause irreparable pain and disappointment for many. How can a natural force of life given to us by the Creator be so necessary yet so painful and difficult? The old cliché, "The only thing that is certain is change," rings more true with each year that passes by, and passes with seemingly increasing speed. Changes that are brought on, sometimes out of the clear blue sky, happen over and over again and we barely notice when we stop long enough to sit and take a short look back at our lives. We sit and wonder where the time went and how we find ourselves in our current situation. The more we think things stay the same, year after year they don't. "Same stuff different day" is an easy, quick response but never entirely true.

Having Butch in my life at this point has changed me significantly. Living for something outside of you can only bring out the good that may have been buried under years of growing cynical thoughts. Caring for something that would die if left to its own devices awakens the spirit, lightens the heart, and gives a seed of meaning to an otherwise mundane life.

Dogs can bring about changes in a person's life that would otherwise be left buried. I'm glad that I have Butch and I wouldn't trade him for anything. He has helped me to grow as a person and as a man. Showing my feelings for Butch is not something I would have ever thought I would do a few years ago. The old "tough guy" routine melted away very quickly once Butch was dropped into my lap. Life changed for me and suddenly it was OK to be myself, to grow up, and to approach life like an adult. I felt as if I didn't have to be all things to all people any longer. I had a new purpose that did not include trying to cram work into every waking hour of the day and night. It did not include trying to do everything to please everyone else at the expense of my own money, time, and energy for the unappreciative crowd that surrounded me. I had a new purpose, which allowed me to step back, slow down, and settle in for a new daily lesson on how to live.

Butch goes everywhere with me. He wants to be with me no matter what mood I'm in and is at my side even now while I'm writing this. He loves me and is not ashamed to show it. He doesn't care what anyone thinks. He loves to be around me no matter what I'm doing and takes advantage of every moment we have together. He can depend on me and he knows it. This gives him a level of comfort that lets him be himself and not be afraid. It's this attitude I see in him that I believe I have learned the most from.

He hasn't missed a meal yet and it's up to me to make sure that he never does. He has filled a void in my life that I never noticed was there. He gave me a new perspective on what is most important to me, not only in the present but also for the future. It's not that I had trouble facing the future before Butch came along. It's just that now, moving into the future with him, it will be much more fun to see what lies ahead for us. The past is further away for me now that Butch is here. My mistakes, missteps, and bad choices although not forgotten do not seem to weigh as much on my mind, leaving me to move forward with more capacity to live life to the fullest.

Oh, I know there are those who might say, "Oh brother, he is really going overboard with this." And for those I can only say that it's true. If you don't own a dog, you can't possibly understand the impact that they can have on your life. If you do own a dog and you can't identify with what I'm saying, then you have not really given your dog a chance to affect you the way that they really can.

I have had a good life and it is, hopefully, far from over but things have drastically changed over these many years and not all for the better. It's a time when society seems to be crumbling before our very eyes; natural disasters are occurring somewhere in the world every few months; terrorists and lunatics are prowling the streets, schools, and malls, killing anyone they come across; government running amok; wars being fought; racism of every kind still dividing countries and people. Yet with all of these things happening around us, there is something about looking into a dog's eyes that calms the worry of the day. It is a peace that can be found there based on an understanding that we as humans have not yet learned.

Dogs have a society all their own, just as we do. There are rich dogs, poor dogs, dogs living on the streets, middle-class dogs, farm dogs, dogs running in gangs, police dogs, fire-fighting dogs – the list goes on and on. It is very easy for us to humanize dogs and somewhat relate our society to the way they have been forced to live also. We can create our own household with dogs, treating them like children all their lives and relating to them better than people in some cases. This may not be the healthiest of answers to the problems we all face in society today but one thing is for sure. Dogs love us and we know it. This unconditional love is the greatest healing emotion a person can feel and whether we get it from a dog or another pet or preferably from another human being, we can't help but feel better about life and ourselves in it. No matter what pains our everyday lives bring or what bad turns the society we live in may take, our dog is there for us. Man and woman's best friend, counting the minutes, waiting at home for us to come through the door. They are the greatest of teachers and the most willing of students. They deserve our thanks, our love, our respect, and our admiration for what they bring to our lives!

Jeff Marginean

Some Great Resources

Everyone has resources. They always make lists and keep track of every little thing they come across, thinking that someday they might be able to use it. It sits around at the bottom of a growing stack of papers and materials, which take up residence in various parts of the house for six months until it finally has a family of other stacks that eventually joins them for a reunion in the garbage can after a complete journey around the house. I hope to spare you some of the pain of moving your growing stack of papers and the little notes that you may be keeping by giving you a good list of places to start when researching or needing some quick answers about your pet. Naturally, I have used these Web sites extensively in researching various issues from toys to toes and have found them to be very helpful. These sites are all great for kids who like animals so don't be afraid to let them surf around each one. I will be sure to update our web site when I come across something that is particularly helpful or interesting!

My Buddy Butch

www.mybuddybutch.com

I will have updates, schedules, monthly tips, and general information available on a timely basis. There is also a blog that Butch and I will be updating regularly with new information. You will also find these and other helpful links on our Web site!

American Kennel Club (AKC)

www.akc.org

This organization is a world of helpful knowledge. From breeders to shows and everything in between including scheduled activities for dogs and families around the country.

Humane Society of the United States

www.hsus.org

This is also a great site with a huge amount of information on adoption programs, religion and animals, and other interesting information on animal care.

Invisible Fence Corporation

www.invisiblefence.com

Great company, great service, it has literally saved Butch's life and removed my worry!

PetSmart

www.petsmart.com

Endless offerings at this place. I have nothing but praise for a great resource and a caring company. They also offer training classes.

PetFinder

www. petfinder.com

This is one fantastic site! This site is a great place to see and adopt a various selection of animals. Adopting a pet can be the best thing that happens to you … and the pet.

Animal Planet

animal.discovery.com

This site is great for inquisitive kids that like to watch Animal Planet on TV. They have pet and wild animal guides, blogs and many more interesting items that you will not find on TV.

Woofboard.com a Boston Terrier Board

www.woofboard.com

All topics about Boston terriers can be found here. This is a great collection of BT lovers that could answer just about any question you may have on the breed!

Acknowledgements

When I started writing this book I had no idea the time, effort, and talent of so many different people would be needed to bring it to a successful completion. There are many people to thank and I am grateful to each of them for their individual contribution and encouragement while walking through this process with me. First, I would like to thank God for the ability He has given me, and the wisdom to begin to use it somewhat correctly. Searching for one's calling can be a lifetime activity for some and my faith has lead me down some strange paths. I am grateful that He never let me get too lost! My Mom has been a great influence on me for giving me the gift of her love that will live with me for the rest of my life. She deserves my thanks for supplying me with a life full of great memories. I want to thank my Dad, Gene Marginean, for giving me Butch in the first place and for passing on to me his unending love for animals.

My brother Jim and sister Jeanne, for letting me disclose some of their past and present. My sister Judy, a teacher and avid reader of books, for her coaching, insight, and valuable advice during this process.

My life-long friend Dave Deremer for being a great example and brother since the first day we met. You have been a steadfast friend.

Father Jay Clark at St. Paul's Catholic Church for sharing your thoughts and biblical knowledge with me. The many people I have come to know over the years at St. Paul's. You have all become a big part of my life and my faith.

Deb Keets for her patient advice and guidance throughout this literary journey and Tim Snider who supervised the copyediting and proof reading.

My friend Rich Kuntz and his family for letting me share part of his story about Brandi.

Ken, Cheryl, Danielle, and Christine Morrison for being the great friends that you are.

Trainers Leslie Jeandrevin and Cheryl Swart-Nist for their patience, great training advice, and friendship. You both have helped me raise Butch right more than you'll ever know. I appreciate you both.

Joe Procario who I have laughed with for years, through good and bad times. No matter what the situation, we could always find something to laugh about.

Joe Lagani for his never failing optimism, and encouragement seeing the potential in any situation. And Lisa Rizzo for being right there, on the spot, willing to help out whenever you are needed. You have all been great help in taking care of the label (Frog & Scorpion Records) while I have been writing this project. You have given me the latitude to be creative on many levels and I thank each of you for your talent and contribution to every project we work on together. You are all true friends.

Professor Samuel Vasbinder Ph.D. Senior Lecturer, Department of English at the University of Akron, for sharing your valued opinion, and gracious in-depth analysis and comment on this project.

Barbara Nowlin, and Maria Schmidt for their valuable detailed critique of the preliminary galley of the book.

All of my friends and associates at the Timken Company for their support and encouragement when they didn't even realize they were giving it.

There are many people who have crossed my path during the time it has taken me to write this book who have contributed to this project without even realizing it – to all of them I say, thank you!

There are many people behind the scenes that have touched these pages in the way of proof reading, editing, and evaluation. Although I cannot possibly know all of your names, you know who you are and I thank you.

I apologize to those individuals who are not mentioned here or those that I may have forgotten.

Finally, I want to thank Butch. Without knowing your existence has made such a difference in many lives, you consistently lighten my days by just being around. Your endless will to make friends with everyone you meet endears you to them all. "Thanks Butch! I don't know how I can ever repay you! Maybe a nice rare steak!

About the Author

Jeff Marginean is a member of the Dog Writers Association of America (DWAA), a new dog dad, musician, music producer, and voting member of the National Academy for Recording Arts and Sciences, Inc., for the Grammy Awards. He is president and CEO of JEMAR Entertainment, Inc., and Frog & Scorpion Records Corporation. He is a mild-mannered process control engineer by day and an author, producer, and artist by night. He lives in a nice, quiet city in Ohio with his dog son Butch and gets his best ideas while mowing the lawn.

Goodbye for now ...

Jeff and Butch